❦ The ❦
Appliqué Garden

Baltimore style with
an English twist

Shirley Bloomfield

TEAMWORK
CRAFTBOOKS

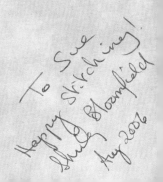

Contents

Contents

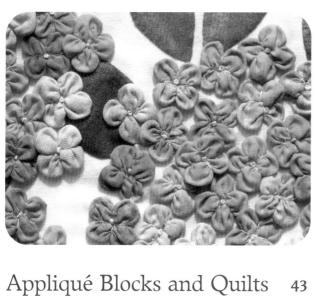

Introduction

In 1992 I saw my first modern Baltimore Album Quilt and I was enthralled by the wonderful blending of foliage, flowers, birds and fruits into stylised wreaths and hearts, and full of admiration for the intricate appliqué and attention to detail – decorative baskets filled with colourful blooms, and cornucopias overflowing with fruit. I was intrigued to find out more about the style. Fortunately help was at hand in the inspirational books written by Elly Sienkiewicz (see Resources, page 79); these not only provided technical advice and designs, but also gave me historical insights into the development of the Baltimore Album style which was popular in America in the mid-nineteenth century. The quilts have a fascinating history, reflecting the culture of the time as well as the importance of family, friendship, religion and civic pride in the lives of the makers. I have had the good fortune to see many of the original Baltimore Album Quilts. A wonderful exhibition in 2004 at The Baltimore Museum of Art showed a stunning collection – almost sensory overload for the viewer!

Inspired by this style, I starting making blocks in the mid-1990s using the traditional designs, but soon I began to design my own blocks. Many of the original Baltimore designs arose out of the images which were available to quilters at the time on china, chintzes and other household items; these images in turn were influenced by classical designs which have been around for centuries. So in a similar way I looked to my environment for design sources.

The flowers and birds in my own garden provided me with an endless source of inspiration. I live in rural Suffolk, and my 500-year-old cottage is surrounded by a large cottage garden; whatever the season, there is always something of interest. It's always exciting to see the first spring bulbs appear and the early shrubs come into bloom. The herbaceous borders in summer are full of colour as delphiniums, campanulas, roses, penstemons and other cottage garden favourites vie for the attention of butterflies and bees. Autumn brings a blaze of colour, as the leaves turn from green to gold, brown and purple. As it's a cottage garden there is also a productive vegetable plot, a small orchard and a wild, woodland area. Here too I can find lots of ideas for appliqué designs.

And of course no cottage garden would be complete without its wildlife. This too changes with the seasons.

The red-breasted robin, doves, blackbirds, colourful great tits and green woodpeckers are frequent all-year-round visitors. Less common are the goldfinches and bullfinches. I am very fortunate to have such a wealth of design sources close at hand, and I hope you will find the photographs of my garden a useful source of ideas even if you do not have your own garden. As a start, look at the colour and shading on petals and leaves before selecting fabrics. I have heard many of my students say they look at fabric in a new light now they have started to appliqué.

I trained as a textile teacher, and after retiring from teaching in High Schools I started teaching workshops for quilters using my own designs. I have developed techniques based on my experience teaching many hundreds of quilters over recent years. My aim is to ensure that techniques will work and that students will

be able to achieve accuracy and success. Several refinements I have made to my techniques have been the results of students' suggestions; it really is a truism that 'by your students you will be taught'!

Through my years of teaching it has been a great privilege to see students blossom and produce beautiful blocks – some moving on to develop their own designs, or at least stamp their individual style on a design by making a few changes. This is something I would encourage you to consider: once you have acquired the basic needle-turning skills, try adapting some of the designs. Perhaps you could make your own flower arrangement in the little *Blue Vase* design (see page 39). Try experimenting with some of the dimensional techniques. I love including dimensional flowers in designs for added texture and interest. A simple technique, such as Suffolk Puffs, can be adapted to create a variety of flowers by using the appropriate colour, size and number of petals. A browse through garden books and catalogues will trigger many possibilities.

I hope you will find this book useful in three ways. First, to learn the basic techniques of needle-turning and gain

confidence in turning sharp points and making smooth curves. Do not be afraid of appliqué! Secondly, it is a useful pattern source for blocks and quilts to perfect your skills. Finally, but by no means least, I hope that the photographs of my garden will encourage you to design your own appliqué and inspire future quilts. Baltimore style with an English flavour has brought me a great deal of pleasure – I hope it will do the same for you!

✧ *How to use this book* ✧

The book has six main sections:

1 The first part is about **getting organised**, and covers choice of fabrics and equipment. There is also useful advice for organising the work area. I would strongly advise checking the suggestions for fabric selection as this is fundamental to success and is relevant for whatever method of appliqué you like to use.

2 The section on **basic techniques** covers the basics of needle-turning and includes step-by-step photographs to help you achieve invisible stitches, sharp points, smooth curves and perfect circles. Even if you are familiar with hand appliqué, you will find this section full of useful tips. The project instructions frequently refer back to this section.

3 The **starter projects** are small projects which include many of the basic techniques.

4 In this section I've included ideas and instructions for **dimensional flowers**, together with some small projects. Further dimensional techniques are included in the individual block designs.

5 The major part of the book is a series of **block and quilt designs** using various appliqué techniques. I've put these in order of difficulty, starting with the

simpler designs. Each one introduces particular techniques and this is indicated at the start of the instructions. The earlier projects also give more detailed instructions for each stage. The full size designs are given at the end of the book. However as the designs do not normally fit onto one page, you will need to make a tracing, matching up on the indicated points to make a complete drawing.

6 The final part of the book focuses on **finishing touches** – taking your appliqué through to a finished project. Ideas for borders, sets, quilting and binding are included. This is a handy reference section for making up quilts whatever techniques you have used to make the top.

Although this book is essentially about hand appliqué, you could adapt many of the designs for machine appliqué and raw-edge appliqué. I have also used the dimensional flowers in a variety of craft projects – try using them in card designs, to decorate fabric-covered box-tops, and as embellishments on garments.

Whatever techniques you like to use for your quilting projects, I hope you will find that the garden photographs will provide inspiration for your own designs and fabric selection.

Getting Organised

Fabrics

Colour is what first attracts most of us to a particular fabric – the bolts of cloth and trays of fat quarters in the quilt shop are enticingly displayed by colour. We spend a great deal of time trying to choose from such a tempting array. However, there are certain types and prints that seem to work best for the method of appliqué I will be showing you in this book.

I always use 100% cotton fabric, the same type used for patchwork and quilting. This weight and fibre work best for needle-turning, as the fabric will crease to give a smooth edge to the appliqué. Look also for fabric that has a reasonably high thread count so that it does not fray a lot. Coarser, more open weave fabrics will fray easily and lead to frustration.

Batiks are my favourite fabrics; not only are they closely woven so they fray very little, but they also come in some wonderful colours and prints which are ideal for achieving shading on leaves and petals. A disadvantage of batiks is that as the fabric is so closely woven, the appliqué stitch tends to sit on the surface instead of snuggling down in the weave of the fabric. However, if you use a very fine thread in a closely-matching colour you can overcome this difficulty.

Besides the weight and the weave of a fabric, the other factor to consider is the printed design. I used to hand-dye fabrics, but I don't any longer as there is now such a wide range of prints which have a hand-dyed appearance. Prints which look like tie-dyed fabric have lovely colour gradations that can lend realism to your appliqué design, so look for textures, 'splashy' prints and random designs rather than regular prints. A checked or spotted green fabric, though it's fun for folk art and naïve designs, will not produce a realistic, natural-looking leaf or stem. Leaf prints are also useful as you can 'fussy-cut' elements: more of that later.

Silk fabrics are more difficult to needle-turn and tend to fray badly. However, you can make them usable by backing them with a very fine iron-on interfacing. Ultrasuede[R], a non-woven fabric with a suede-like appearance, is helpful for very small shapes.

Neutral-coloured backgrounds in subtle prints enhance the appliqué. Again these should be 100% cotton so that they work well with the needle-turning technique, but avoid fabrics with heavily-printed designs that almost create a painted surface, as these are hard to stitch through. For my first pieces of hand appliqué I chose a plain cream as I thought that was necessary to show off the appliqué. Having only seen illustrations of some of the original Baltimore Album Quilts which were worked on a plain fabric, I thought this was the way to go. However, when I later saw modern appliqué quilts with patterned background fabrics I liked the effect better. It was less stark, but of course the pattern must not be too dominant, otherwise it will conflict with the appliqué.

Look at the background fabrics that I have used for the projects in this book for ideas. A dark background can also be used with stunning effect; for instance, light-coloured flowers really glow on a deep blue background. I will give you some tips later on for working on a dark background (see page 54).

To wash or not to wash!

There is always a debate about this, with different stitchers having their own preferences. Personally I do wash all my fabrics before using them for appliqué; I have seen too many fabrics 'bleed' to risk not pre-washing.

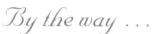

Washing will remove excess dye and sizing. I wash in a 40° synthetic programme (with no washing detergent), adding a 'dye-catcher' sheet to pick up any unfixed colour; I then iron the fabric while it's still damp to produce a crease-free finish. I've found that if a commercially-dyed fabric still seems to bleed dye, rinsing it in a solution of Retayne™ fixes the colour.

How much should I buy?

A fat quarter will go a long way when you're stitching this kind of appliqué. It's better to have a lot of small pieces in a wide range of colours than a few large pieces. If you spot an interesting fabric you like, buy a piece for the stash – you will find a use for it in due course.

If I go shopping for a specific colour I need I can never find it. So, best to be prepared!

Store your appliqué fabrics by colour for easy access. You can then see if you are low on a particular colour range and can re-stock when you next visit a quilt shop or show.

By the way . . .

For all the instructions in this book, and most of the requirements, I have given imperial measurements only. Most quilters are used to working in imperial, and – unlike many other patchwork techniques – accurate seam allowances are not critical for hand appliqué. The only exceptions are when there are larger amounts of fabric in the requirements lists, when I've given both the imperial and the metric equivalent so that you know how much to buy, and when I've included the finished sizes of the projects.

Equipment

Threads

To state the obvious – to produce fine stitching, you need a fine thread! My preferred thread is YLI™ #100 silk thread; it comes in a wide range of colours. Start with basic neutral colours in dark, medium and light tones as these will blend in with many appliqué fabrics. Build up your collection with different colours as the need arises. As an alternative thread you might prefer a cotton #60 machine embroidery thread; this too comes in a wide range of colours and is nearly as fine as the silk thread. Silk is easy to sew with if you bear the following tips in mind:

- Cut the thread the length from your fingertip to your elbow.

- Run the thread across beeswax to prevent it from tangling while you're stitching.

- Tie the thread in the needle as described below to prevent the thread from coming out of the needle. The thread is so fine that the knot passes easily through the fabric.

a   Loop the short end of the the thread over itself.

b   Insert the needle through the loop.

c   Pull the loop over the eye of the needle.

d   Pull the short end of the thread to tighten the knot.

e   Pull the long end of the thread to bring the knot up to the eye of the needle.

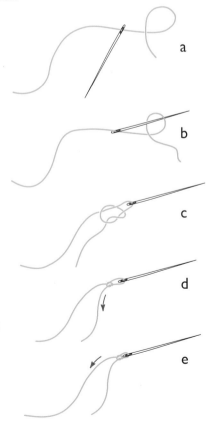

Needles

I first learnt to needle-turn using a short #10 Between needle. However, once I was introduced to #11 Straw needles I found the needle-turning technique much easier and quicker. Although these needles are made in the UK, they are very hard to find here, but I have managed to track some down (see Resources on page 79). Straw needles are very fine and long, and the extra length makes it easier to manipulate the needle. They do bend slightly with prolonged use, and once your needle is completely boomerang-shaped it's time to pick a fresh one!

Other needles you might like to experiment with are Sharps #11 or Milliners #10.

A needle threader is very useful for helping you to thread such fine needles.

Pins

Over the years I have tried many types of pins for appliqué. The ideal pin needs to be short and fine, with a smooth head for comfortable handling. The pins that seem to answer all these requirements are the appliqué pins made by Clover™; they are sold in little plastic boxes, but I recommend that you make a mini pincushion just for these pins, as it's much easier to pick them up from a pincushion than from the container. Also, it's easy to spill the container, resulting in pins all over the work area ...

Turning sticks

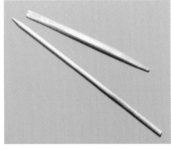

These are not specialist quilting gadgets, but are items that you will find in grocery/household departments. One of these little bamboo skewers – about 4in long, with a pointed end – is ideal for turning under the seam allowance when you are needle-turning. Another kind of stick you will find useful is one with a flat end: this is brilliant for turning corners. This type is no longer manufactured, though, so you may need to whittle one of the regular sticks to produce a flat end.

Scissors

Small, sharp-to-the-point scissors are essential for accurate cutting. With blunt scissors it is easy to exert too much pressure and cut too far into the seam allowance!

Small, sharp paper scissors with pointed blades will help you to produce accurate templates. Your final appliqué shape can only be as good as the template!

Rotary-cutting equipment

A rotary-cutter plus cutting mat and quilter's ruler make cutting bias strips, blocks and borders much easier. A 15in-square quilter's ruler is useful for cutting background squares and squaring up blocks when they are finished.

Markers/drawing equipment

A well-sharpened pencil can be used for marking stems on the background.

A Clover™ white marking pen (fine) is brilliant for drawing round templates onto fabric; the line is fine, but shows up even on light fabrics. The marks disappear as soon as they come in contact with either an iron or water, which is a great advantage if part of the marked line cannot be turned under completely when you're needle-turning a shape; marks made by other types of marking pen cannot be removed so easily.

A Pigma™ 0.1 pen is useful for inking permanently on fabrics and for making labels. It's also good for making overlays (more of that later).

A hera (a Japanese marking tool) is useful for marking quilting lines on fabric. This clever tool leaves a sharp crease on the fabric so that there are no lines to erase.

Supplies for template making

Freezer paper is ideal for making templates which can be re-used many times before they lose their adhesive properties. You will find that the freezer paper has a matt, papery finish on one side, and a shiny, waxy finish on the other. The shapes of your templates are always traced onto the matt side, and once they are cut out the shapes are laid shiny side down onto the fabrics and pressed; the slightly waxy surface makes the template stick to the fabric.

A circle template is invaluable for drawing circles on fabric as well as for making card templates.

Pre-cut Mylar™ circles are wonderful for creating perfect, accurate circles for berries, grapes, cherries etc (see Resources on page 79). Mylar™ is a heat-resistant plastic; don't confuse it with ordinary template plastic, which distorts when it is heated. This is an important point as the fabric is gathered over the circle and then pressed with a hot iron (see page 17). You can of course make your own circles, but it is very difficult to cut tiny, accurate, smooth circles!

Pressing equipment

A small travel iron or the Clover™ Mini Iron is useful for ironing on templates and for pressing small areas. A Teflon™ pressing sheet (or baking sheet) can be used to protect the work when you are giving it a final press. It's also useful for protecting the ironing board and iron when you are using fusible web (see page 70).

Your work area

A comfortable working environment will not only increase the pleasure of sewing but will help you to work faster and more accurately.

How well can you see?

Good light is essential. Natural daylight is good for colour-matching and choosing fabrics. If you have to sew by artificial light and haven't a lamp which simulates natural light, you might find it best to choose your fabrics in the day for sewing later.

A portable lamp that can be angled in the correct position for you will be the most useful. Ott-Lite™ make a portable model that is useful for taking about and which folds up for safe carrying. Avoid light bulbs which get hot, as after a while you will find it uncomfortable to stitch under the heat.

A larger view?

I also always sew under a magnifier; I find that I can see what I'm doing more clearly, so the stitching is quicker and there is less strain on the eyes. Various magnifying aids are available, ranging from clip-on lenses which can be worn with regular spectacles through to magnifiers which clip to the table or lamp. It's worth trying a magnifier to see whether it will help you to stitch more comfortably.

Are you sitting comfortably?

I'm not a medical person but I do know that when we're sewing for long stretches of time (or even for a short while) we all need to be careful to avoid stress in the neck, shoulders and back.

It helps to have a chair with good back support. I use a good-quality office chair which also allows me to swivel round to reach things. Raising your feet on a little footstool also produces a more comfortable posture for stitching. Some appliqué stitchers like to work with the stitching on a lap tray supported by the edge of the table. Make sure, too, that you take regular breaks from your stitching even if it's just getting up to iron on some templates. If you bear these points in mind, it will mean that you can stitch for longer and get greater enjoyment from the work.

A place for everything?

Organising your work space well will help you to work more efficiently, be more productive and reduce the frustration of looking for missing things! Even if you are not naturally a tidy person it does pay to keep the bits and pieces of your appliqué organised in some way. This kind of work requires a lot of small templates and pieces of fabric that can easily get lost.

The system I use is to keep all the fabrics for a particular project in a small basket together with a folder containing all the templates, design etc. While I'm stitching I keep another small box or basket beside me, into which I can drop the templates after I've removed them from the appliqué shapes. I also have a small tray beside me on which I have my turning sticks, small pin-cushion, small scissors, beeswax, needle-case, white marking pen and the threads I am using for that particular block or project. This way, everything I am using at the time is close to hand, and not getting swept onto the floor or otherwise mislaid. When a project is completed I keep all the templates, pattern windows, overlay and design in a large envelope filed for possible future use. (Remember that the templates etc can be re-used many times.)

The basic techniques that I cover here are used for the projects throughout the book. (You'll find particular techniques used for individual projects under the instructions for those projects.) The general technique involves using freezer paper templates on top of appliqué shapes which are needle-turned in place. Alternatively, you can draw around the templates, then remove each template before the shape is needle-turned in position. I explain both methods in this section.

Before you begin the appliqué, you need to find the centre of the background fabric; this will help you to position the design and the appliqué correctly. Fold the fabric in half vertically and lightly finger-press. (Do not iron the centre lines as you will find it difficult to remove the creases later.) Mark the crease with small tacking stitches, using a light-coloured thread that will show up on your background. Avoid dark-coloured threads, which sometimes leave marks on the background fabric. Re-fold the background in half horizontally, matching the two halves of the tacked line, and finger-press; mark the creased line with tacking as before. It's worth taking a bit of care at this stage to ensure that the centre lines are accurately marked with tacking; it will save problems later when you are positioning the appliqué pieces.

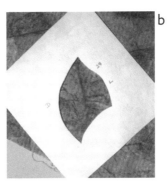

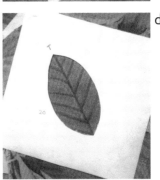

Preparation

1 Prepare the freezer paper template

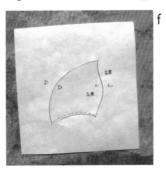

Use a sharp pencil to trace the shape from the design sheet onto the matt side of the freezer paper.

Number the template and beside the template (**a**).
When an edge is covered by an adjacent shape it will not need to be turned under; mark any such edges with a dotted line. The example I've used in the photograph is leaf #28 from the *Woodpecker* design on page 67.

2 Make a 'pattern window'

Carefully cut the template out of its surrounding freezer paper, leaving a hole the exact shape of the template which you can then use as a pattern window. (You may prefer to use a small craft knife rather than scissors to cut out the templates.) This hole or window is used to help you choose the most effective area of print to use

for a shape; for example, photograph **b** shows a leaf template positioned on a good area of a particular fabric, and photograph **c** shows the same template positioned on an area of the fabric that doesn't work nearly so well. Leaf prints can be very useful, but make sure that the veins run in the correct direction; if you mark the tip of the leaf shape on the window and on the template (**d**), this will help you to get the direction right. If I'm trying to keep the light falling consistently across the design I mark the light and dark edges on each shape on the design sheet with L and D; you can then use the same notation on the templates and windows to avoid confusion (**e**).

3 Prepare the appliqué shapes

Use the pattern window to select the position for your template. Drop the template back in the window (**f**), remove the window, and iron the template onto the right side of the fabric (**g**).

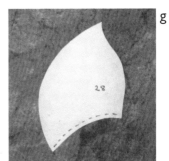

Use a hot iron (cotton setting) and a firm surface. Cut out the shape, adding a scant ⅛in seam allowance (h).

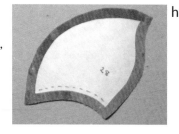

h

Method 1

1 Position the shape on the background

Slide the prepared shape under the overlay (see page 18 for how to make an overlay). The photograph (i) shows leaf #8 from the *Woodpecker* design being positioned. Line up the template carefully with the drawing on the overlay.

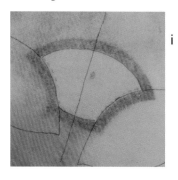

i

2 Pin the shape in position

Hold the shape in place while you fold back the overlay, then secure the shape with two pins in the seam allowance (j). (Do not pin through the paper template – this will shift the shape out of position.)

j

3 Tack/baste the shape in place

Work a few tacking/basting stitches ¼in inside the paper edge to hold the fabric shape in position, then remove the pins (k).

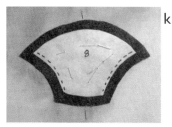

k

Method 2

1 Draw round the template

If you do not like to have the paper template in place while you are needle-turning, an alternative method is to draw round the edge of the template using the fine white marking pen (a). It helps to place a piece of fine sandpaper under the fabric while you are drawing round the template; the fabric will then

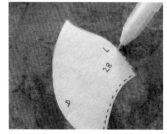

a

stay flat and will not shift. If an edge is to be covered by another appliqué shape, do not draw on this edge; leaving it unmarked will remind you that the edge does not need to be needle-turned. It's easy otherwise to get carried away and sew all round a shape, forgetting that some edges should be left raw as they will be covered by other shapes.

2 Cut out the shape

Now cut the shape out, leaving a slightly smaller seam allowance than you would for Method 1, since the drawn line is part of the seam allowance (b).

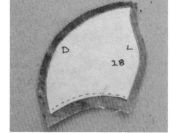

b

3 Pin the shape in position

Keep the freezer paper in place while you position the shape on the background with the aid of the overlay (as for Method 1). As before, pin in the seam allowance only; remove the freezer paper at this stage.

4 Tack/baste the shape in place

Work a line of running stitch ¼in inside the drawn line. Note the undrawn edge (c).

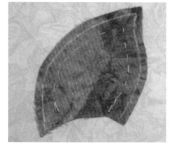

c

5 Needle-turn

Follow the instructions for needle-turning, but note that you will be turning under both the seam allowance and the drawn line as you stitch. You will find, too, that in the needle-turning instructions (see page 13), I've included some extra tips for working with the drawn line method.

It's worth trying both methods to find which works best for you. Some of my students prefer keeping the paper in place, and others prefer the drawn line method. When I started I preferred keeping the paper on top, but at that time the white marking pens were not available. The advantage of these pens is that not only do they produce a fine line on virtually any colour fabric, but also the line is easily removed by ironing (or water). Therefore if you have not entirely tucked the line out of sight you can easily remove any traces. Read the instructions that come with the pen and bear in mind that the line does not show up until after a few seconds – don't be tempted to draw over several times as you will end up with a messy line!

Perfecting the stitch —
ten steps to success!

For the photographs in these instructions, I've used a thread in a contrasting colour so that you can see exactly what I'm doing; obviously when you are working, you will be using a thread that matches your fabric as closely as possible so that your stitches are as invisible as you can make them.

1 Hold the work with the edge to be appliquéd facing away from you. Right-handed sewers will be stitching from right to left. (If you are left-handed, you will need to follow the same stitching technique but work from left to right.)

2 Make a knot at the end of the thread, then work a small stitch under the shape to get started (**a**).

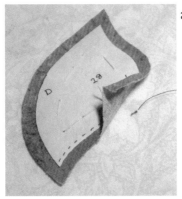

3 Stroke under about ¾in of the seam allowance, either with the side of the needle or by using a small turning stick (**b**). Twist the stick to help roll the edge under. You need to make a curving arc action in an anti-clockwise (counter-clockwise) direction with either the needle or the stick, so that any fullness in the seam allowance is pulled back behind where you are stitching. You need to turn the edge under so that only a small sliver of fabric remains beyond the freezer paper; if you are using the drawn line technique, you will need to turn under the line as well as the seam allowance (**c**). Finger-press the turned-under edge firmly; frequent finger-pressing helps to 'tame' the turned edge.

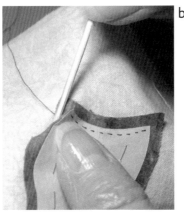

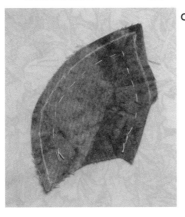

4 Bring the needle up through the folded edge (**d**).

5 Keeping the needle perpendicular, insert it into the background against the appliqué edge, opposite the place where the thread emerges from the folded edge (**e**).

6 Swing the needle up so that it travels a short distance in the background then comes up through the background to just catch the opposite fold in the appliqué (**f**). It helps to keep your left thumb just ahead of the needle to hold the edge down.

7 The length of stitch you take on the background fabric depends on the situation and how comfortable you feel with the stitch. I find that beginners sometimes make quite big stitches (about 6 stitches to the inch) or extremely small stitches (almost stitching on the spot) until they get into the rhythm. An average size for most situations is about 15 stitches to the inch. Pull the thread away from the edge (**g**); this helps to prevent puckering. Your first stitch is now complete. Repeat the process from step 5. After each stitch I tend to finger-press the edge to keep it flat and smooth.

8 You will need to keep sweeping under the edge as necessary as you work your way round the shape. On fairly straight edges you will be able to turn under about an inch of seam allowance at a time; on curved shapes you will need to make more frequent adjustments to maintain a smoothly-curved edge.

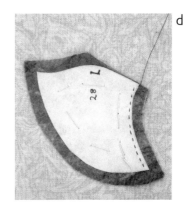

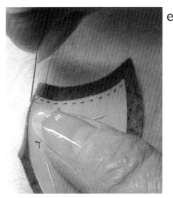

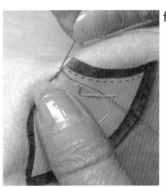

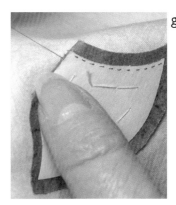

9 Check the back of the work. The stitches should resemble small, straight, close-together running stitches (**h**). My stitches tend to be very small – you do not need to make them as small as shown in the photograph, except when you're stitching very tight inner curves. I stitched this sample with dark red thread on a plain light green fabric in the hope that the stitches would show up clearly; you will see, though, that when I'm working in the fine YLI™ #100 silk thread the stitches are still barely visible (**i**)!

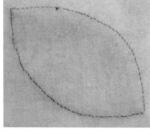

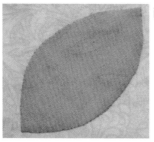

10 To fasten off the thread, take the needle through to the back and work a couple of tiny back stitches in the background under the appliqué.

As with all hand skills, your technique will improve with practice. Here are a few tips if you are having problems.

Problem: Uneven appliquéd edges.

a (back of work)

Solution: This is often the result of too big a gap between the stitches (**a**): the needle is not re-entering the background directly opposite the place where it emerged in the appliqué shape. If there are big gaps between the stitches the edge is not held down sufficiently, which will lead to an uneven edge and possibly some fraying at inner curves.

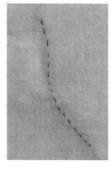

Problem: Slanting stitches on the back of the work, causing a loose, uneven edge (**b**).

b (back of work)

Solution: This happens when you hold the needle in a slanting position as though you are hemming. We are so used to hemming that it needs a conscious effort to hold the needle in a different way. Hold the needle in a more upright position as it enters the background, and keep the needle parallel with the edge as you travel a short distance in the background.

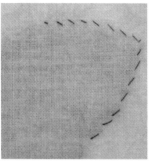

h *Problem:* The stitch shows on the right side.

c

Solution: It is not necessary for your stitches to be completely invisible; tiny, even stitches look good too. However, using a fine thread (see page 8) in a toning colour or an exact colour match helps tremendously. Make sure that you are only taking a thread or two on the appliqué edge and that the stitch does not extend beyond the appliqué shape – this leads to 'hairy' edges! The leaf shown here (**c**) was partly stitched deliberately taking a little too much of the appliqué edge. You can see the difference further along when the needle only just catches the folded edge – once again, although I used a contrasting thread, the stitch is barely visible. If I had used a regular fabric rather than a batik for this example, the stitch would have disappeared completely into the weave of the fabric.

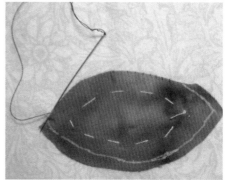

Problem: The stitching puckers.

Solution: You may be pulling the stitches too tight, but what is more likely is that you are pulling the thread backwards after making a stitch. This is the way we are used to sewing, so it's a hard habit to change. If you pull the thread away from the edge at right angles, this will prevent the work from puckering – also, if you get into the habit of automatically finger-pressing the edge after making a stitch or two, that helps to keep the edge flat.

Inner curves

1 If you are using the drawn line method you can clip to the line if necessary (**a**). If you are keeping the freezer paper template on top, clip half the depth of the seam allowance (**b**). Depending on the acuteness of the curve you may need to make

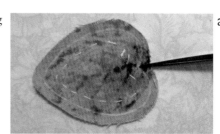

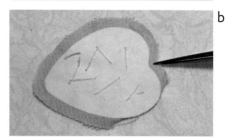

several clips (**c**). Once you have clipped the curve, swing the edge under with the turning stick; the stick works very well on inner curves and enables you to achieve a smooth edge (**d**). If the edge will not turn under sufficiently, make an additional clip until it lies flat, or make the clips slightly deeper.

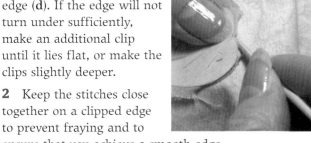

2 Keep the stitches close together on a clipped edge to prevent fraying and to ensure that you achieve a smooth edge.

Outer curves

1 On outer curves there is no need to make any clips in the seam allowance; the seam allowance is so small that any fullness can be accommodated within the turned edge. If you find that the edge will not turn under smoothly, you can reduce the seam allowance slightly.

2 I prefer to use the needle rather than a turning stick for turning under outer curves. If necessary on tight curves you can use the point of the needle both to pull the seam allowance under and to adjust it into place to achieve a smooth line; do this with care, though, as you do not want to pluck and fray the edge. Ease the edge under a small amount at a time; this may mean that you will have to adjust the edge every stitch or so on a very tight curve. On tight curves the stitches need to be small and close together so that the edge is well anchored and the shape of the appliqué stays accurate.

Inner points

1 You will need to clip the seam allowance at an inner point. Mark the position of the cut with the white marking pen (**a**) – as well as showing you exactly where to cut, using the white pen also helps to prevent the fabric from fraying around the cut. (It's often convenient to mark any cuts when you are preparing the shapes before tacking them in position.) Do not make the cut at this stage!

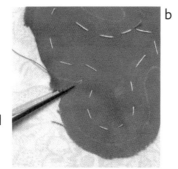

2 Stitch to about ½in away from the inner point. Clip the seam on the line you have marked, clipping almost to the edge of the paper. If you are using a drawn line you can make the final cut up to the drawn line since the line will be turned under (**b**). Use the stick to turn the seam under and continue stitching towards the base of the inner point (**c**). Keep the stitches small and close – there is little seam allowance here.

3 Turn under the adjacent side of the point (**d**), pulling the stick down at the base to give a sharp inner point. At this stage you may have to clip another thread or two at the base if the edge will not turn sufficiently.

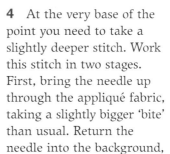

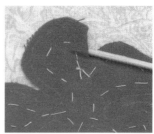

4 At the very base of the point you need to take a slightly deeper stitch. Work this stitch in two stages. First, bring the needle up through the appliqué fabric, taking a slightly bigger 'bite' than usual. Return the needle into the background, slanting the needle well under the edge (**e**). Put your left thumb over the stitch as you pull the thread tightly (this prevents puckering). This slightly bigger stitch will disappear into the fabric and firmly secure the base of the point.

5 Start stitching up the second side of the point. Work the stitch in two stages so you do not pluck out the minuscule seam allowance. Also make the stitches small and close together for great security. Make the first two or three stitches away from the point in this way, and then you will be safe to continue stitching as normal (**f**).

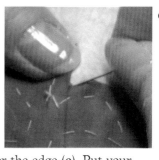

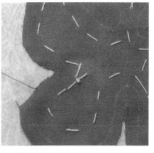

6 If you are keeping the freezer paper in place as you needle-turn, while you are learning you may find it helpful to peel back the freezer paper after stitching the first side so that you can see more clearly what you are doing at the inner point.

When you are stitching a long inner curve, divide the seam allowance evenly between the edges (**g**).

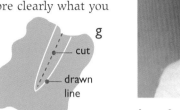

Outer points

Working with outer points can sometimes make appliqué stitchers anxious, but I think that if you use either of these methods, you will find points easier than stitching tight outer curves. Here are a few tips to reduce stress levels.

Method 1

1 Needle-turn along to the point, stopping a 'smidgeon' past the corner if you are using freezer paper on top (**a**). If you are unsure of the technical term 'smidgeon,' in this instance I mean the width of the needle – in other words, it is very small! If you are using a drawn line, stop just before the line (**b**). Make sure that the stitches you work as you approach the corner are small, for extra security.

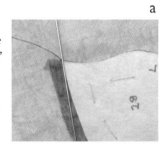

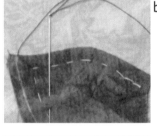

2 Hold the work firmly between the 3rd and 4th fingers on your left hand to produce a bit of tension on the background fabric (**c**).

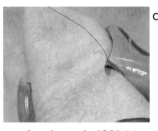

3 Pick up the corner on the point of the needle (**d**), and swing the seam allowance under through 180° (**e**). The needle will now be pushed firmly against the first line of stitching. Carefully remove the needle, and pull gently on the thread to re-align the point, which may

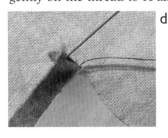

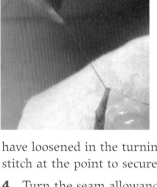

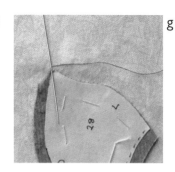

have loosened in the turning process (**f**). Work a small stitch at the point to secure it (**g**).

4 Turn the seam allowance under on the second side of the point and continue stitching as usual.

Method 2

An alternative method for turning points is to use a flat-ended stick; this type of stick makes it much easier to turn a corner. (If you have problems obtaining a stick with a flat end, you could whittle a rounded stick.) Follow Method 1 above to the end of stage 2. Hold the stick as shown and push the point under (**a**), flattening the stick against the background as you turn (**b**). Push the stick down inside the point a couple of times to smooth out any turnings which may have got bunched up. Re-align the point as before (**c**) and work a small stitch at the point. It works well to use the flat end of the stick to turn under some of the seam allowance along the second side of the point, too, before continuing the appliqué (**d**).

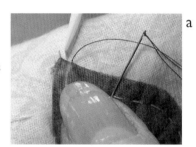

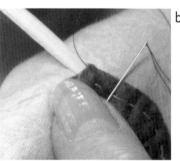

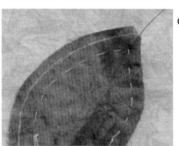

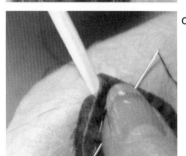

Acute outer points

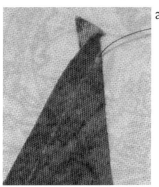
a

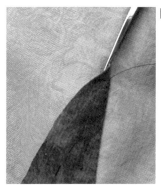
b

1 When you are stitching an acute point (**a**) it's useful to remove some of the seam allowance after stitching the first side of the point; doing this reduces bulk and helps to create a sharper point. Use small, very sharp-pointed scissors; slide the scissor points under the shape and trim a sliver off the seam allowance (**b**).

2 Even if you do not trim the seam allowance, you may find it necessary to turn the point in two stages (**c** and **d**).

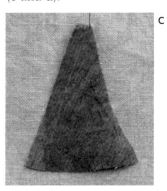
c

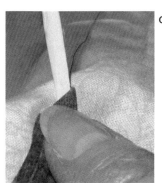
d

Perfect circles

a

1 Circles feature widely in Baltimore appliqué, whether as flower centres, berries or fruits, so it's useful to be able to appliqué an accurate circle. It helps to use a pre-cut circle; the Mylar™ ones (**a**) that I use come in a variety of sizes and are reusable (see Resources on page 79). Alternatively you can cut your own from cardboard but you need to cut accurately.

2 Cut your fabric circle ½in larger in diameter than the finished size. So, for example, for a ¼in finished circle the fabric circle will need to be ¾in diameter; a ½in finished circle will need a 1in diameter fabric circle. A circle template (**b**) is very handy for marking fabric circles.

b

3 Without securing the thread either at the beginning or the end of the stitching line, work a line of small running stitches ⅛in inside the outer edge of the fabric circle (**c**).

c

4 Position the plastic circle centrally on the wrong side of the fabric circle, then hold both ends of the thread and pull them up together tightly (**d**). Press the circle firmly on the back with a hot iron; if you wish you can paint a little spray starch on the wrong side before pressing, as this helps to produce a sharp shape.

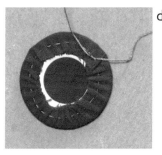
d

5 Ease back the gathering thread a little so that you can remove the plastic circle – tweezers are useful for this operation. Gently pull up the gathers again to return the fabric to the original shape (**e**).

e

6 Appliqué the circle in position using small stitches.

7 The seam allowances will pad the shape slightly, but if you wish you can push in a little wadding before completing the appliqué to provide a little extra padding.

Overlays

An overlay is used to position the appliqué accurately on the background without having to mark the design itself on the background. It's very useful for multi-layered appliqué designs; if you draw the full design on the background for this kind of work, any interior lines are hidden once you have stitched down the first layer. Using an overlay means that the outline of the design is always visible.

To make the overlay I use a lightweight interfacing; it needs to be fairly transparent so that you can easily trace the lines of the design onto it. Be careful which interfacing you use, though, as many have built-in stretch and are too soft for using as overlays; you need a reasonably firm but see-through type (see Resources on page 79).

1 Tape the design onto your work surface, then tape the corners of the interfacing to the work surface too so that nothing moves while you are tracing. With a fine black liner, trace the design – including the centre lines – onto the interfacing.

 TIP *It's a good idea to mark TOP at the top of the overlay; this way you won't make the mistake then of reversing the overlay when you come to attach it to the background fabric.*

---

2 Position the overlay on the background fabric so that the centre lines match. Pin the centre and the ends of the centre lines while you securely tack the overlay in position along the top edge (**a**). When you are not using the overlay it can be rolled up and pinned at the top of the work (**b**).

b

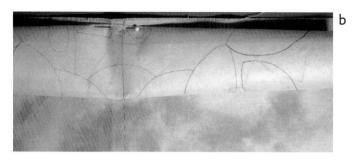

Final thought

This description of the basic appliqué techniques may sound a little daunting – especially if you are a beginner. Don't be put off, though; I have covered the techniques in plenty of detail deliberately. Through my years of experience teaching these techniques to many hundreds of students, I've seen some of the problems which may be encountered; if you do encounter any of these pitfalls, I hope that the suggestions I've given in the instructions for working the needle-turning will help you to overcome them. The most important thing, though, is to practise, and not be disheartened if your first efforts are not as good as you hope. I show my very first piece of appliqué to students so that they can see that we all have to start somewhere! Aim for even stitches that hold the appliquéd edge securely in place rather than total invisibility; this will come with practice.

The other advice I would offer is not to start with anything too challenging. Start simple, gain confidence and move forward. The *Hydrangeas* on page 44 would make a simple first block as an introduction to needle-turned appliqué.

a

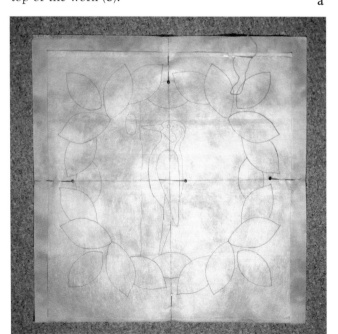

Starter Projects

❦ Project 1 ❦

Oak and Acorn Papercut

Papercuts are a good starting point for practising needle-turning. As you stitch this simple design, based on oak leaves and acorns, you will be able to practise inner and outer curves as well as points. In the Victorian language of flowers, acorns symbolise longevity and oak leaves courage. So have courage as you get started on your first needle-turned design! I worked the original in a batik fabric; if you are a beginner, choose a similar type of cotton fabric that is easy to work in, and avoid fabrics that are likely to fray a lot.

Techniques used

~ cutwork appliqué

~ needle-turned inner and outer curves

~ outer points

FINISHED SIZE: the centre block measures 8½in (22cm) square. The cushion measures approx 16in (41cm) square

The full-size template for this project is on page 80

What you will need

~ 9in square background fabric

~ 9in square appliqué fabric for the papercut design

~ 8 x 16in fabric for the corner triangles

~ ½yd (45cm) fabric for the border and cushion backing

~ silk thread or alternative fine thread to match the appliqué fabric

~ freezer paper for the template

~ for quilting the cushion front:

    18in square low-loft wadding

    18in square backing fabric

~ three small buttons to fasten the cushion cover (or you can make fabric ties if you prefer)

Preparation

Cutwork appliqué is a useful time-saving technique. The appliqué and background fabrics are cut to the same size, then layered with both fabrics right side up and the appliqué fabric on top. For marking the design you can use either the technique of ironing on the freezer paper template, or the drawn line method (see page 12). The layers are tacked together within the shape and the appliqué fabric is then cut away a little at a time as you needle-turn round the shape; by working in this way you don't need to make any placement marks on the background fabric, or to use an overlay. Another advantage of this method is that very thin or complicated shapes are easy to manage, as you only cut out a small section of the shape at a time, just before stitching – less risk of the shape disintegrating before it is appliquéd!

1 To find the centre of the appliqué fabric fold the square in half vertically and finger-press; re-fold it in half horizontally and finger-press.

2 Trace the oak leaf template on page 80 (including the centre lines) onto the matt side of the freezer paper; cut out the shape carefully.

3 Position the freezer paper template centrally on the right side of the appliqué fabric, matching the centre lines; iron the freezer paper in place (**a**).

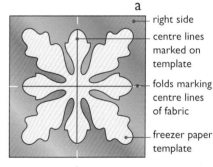

a
— right side
— centre lines marked on template
— folds marking centre lines of fabric
— freezer paper template

4 Now is the time to decide whether you want to keep the freezer paper on top and use it as a guide for the needle-turning, or whether you draw round the template and remove the paper before appliquéing (see page 12). If you decide on the drawn line method, at this point draw around the template – it helps to do this on a cutting mat or sandpaper so that the fabric does not move.

5 Pin the appliqué fabric square to the right side of the background square (**b**). (Remember to pin on the fabric areas only and not through the paper template.)

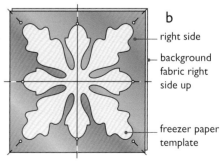

b
— right side
— background fabric right side up
— freezer paper template

6 If you have drawn round the template, remove the freezer paper at this stage and work a line of running stitches ¼in inside the drawn line to tack the two fabrics together (**c**). If you are using the alternative method and keeping the paper template in place while needle-turning, tack the freezer paper shape in place, ¼in inside the edge (**d**).

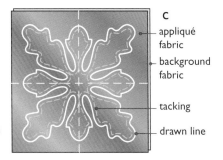

c
— appliqué fabric
— background fabric
— tacking
— drawn line

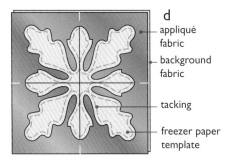

d
— appliqué fabric
— background fabric
— tacking
— freezer paper template

Appliqué

1 To start off, cut the top appliqué fabric centrally between a leaf and an acorn; try to leave the same amount of seam allowance on each side (**e**). Continue cutting round the inner curve up to the first corner, leaving an ⅛in seam allowance. (With the drawn line method you could have slightly less seam allowance – see page 12.)

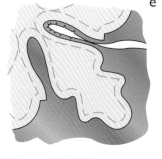

e

2 Clip the inner curves as necessary (see page 14). Follow the basic instructions (see pages 13-14) to needle-turn the raw edge, leaving just enough fabric beyond the freezer paper on which to stitch. Do not stitch through the paper. If you have removed the template, turn the edge under as you stitch so that the drawn line is just under the edge.

I suggest that you start the needle-turning at point X on the template. You can then stitch round the inner curve and up towards the first corner; stop stitching ½in from the corner.

3 Cut away the appliqué fabric around the acorn as before.

4 The next stage is a bit of a challenge, as you have an outer corner followed immediately by an inner corner!

You will need to snip the inner corner before turning the outer corner (see page 15).

5 Continue in this way around the papercut, cutting out the shape a few inches at a time and needle-turning the trimmed edge.

6 Once the whole shape has been appliquéd, remove any tacking (and the template if relevant) as shown in diagram **f**; press the appliqué on the reverse side.

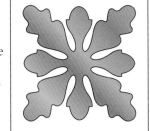

f

To border the block

(Note: I've included ¼in seam allowances in the measurements given here)

1 Cut two 7in squares from the fabric you have chosen for the corners. Cut each square diagonally; you now have four triangles which will become the corners of your finished design.

From the border fabric, cut two strips each 12½ x 2½in for the side borders, and two 16½ x 2½in strips for the top and bottom borders.

2 Add one triangle to each side of the appliqué design as shown (**g**). Press the seams towards the triangles, and trim the work to an accurate 12½in square.

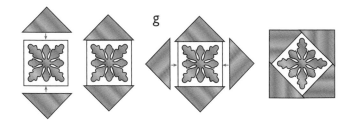

g

3 Sew on the shorter side borders first (**h**), then add the borders at the top and bottom (**i**); press the seams towards the outer edges of the cushion cover.

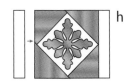

h

i

Quilting

1 To make a template for the corner design, trace onto freezer paper the shape marked by a dotted line on the appliqué template. Position the template in one corner triangle and lightly iron it in place (**j**); mark the outline with a quilting pencil.

j

Remove the template, then repeat the process in each of the remaining corners (**k**).

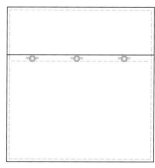

k

2   Layer the backing square, the wadding and the appliqué design to make a quilt 'sandwich' (see page 74).

3   Outline the papercut block design with hand quilting, working about ⅛in away from the appliqué shape. Work a second line around the design about ⅜in beyond the first one.

4   Quilt the corner design, adding a further line of quilting on the inner edge of the design (**l**).

l

5   Trim the work to an accurate 16½in square.

Finishing

1   For the cushion back, cut one piece of fabric 16½ x 7½in, and one piece 16½ x 12¼in. Make a hem on one long edge of each piece by pressing under first ¼in and then ¾in to the wrong side; machine the hems in place (**m**).

m

2   Lay the appliqué design right side up on a flat surface, then position the two hemmed rectangles on top, right sides down, so that the hemmed edges overlap and all the raw edges align (**n**).

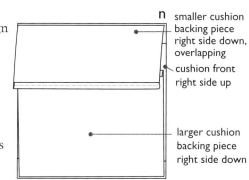

n   smaller cushion backing piece right side down, overlapping

cushion front right side up

larger cushion backing piece right side down

Machine-stitch a ¼in seam all the way around the edge. Trim the wadding away from the seam allowance at the corners, then turn the cushion cover right side out.

3   Roll out the edge of the cushion and tack this edge in place, or pin it (inserting the pins at right angles). Work a line of machine top-stitch ¼in from the edge.

4   Work three buttonholes on the lower section of the cushion backing, stitching on the hemmed area for extra strength. Sew buttons onto the upper backing section so that they correspond (**o**). Alternatively you could make matching ties to fasten the back opening, or use Velcro™.

o

Now your project is complete!

✍ Variations ✍

You can use this block in many different ways; here are some further ideas.

Counterchange, version 1

1   Seam two triangles to create a background square – choose a light and a dark tone for maximum effect, or perhaps two contrasting colours.

2   Seam the appliqué square in the same way.

3   Layer the squares and work the appliqué as described in the project instructions.

4   Join four squares as shown above.

Counterchange, version 2

This is simpler version. Alternate the light and dark tones as shown on the right; add borders to make a small quilt or cushion.

∽ *Project 2* ∽

Apples

This simple apple and leaf motif can be used in a number of ways. Here I have used six blocks to make a small wall quilt which would fit well in a kitchen or dining room; you could use just three or four blocks to make a smaller quilt as another starter project. Or how about using the motif on tablemats or a runner?

Now that you have practised needle-turning with the papercut design, here is a chance to experiment with simple shading, using the design on your fabric to create shaded apples. Apples come in a range of colours: check the greengrocery or a gardening book for ideas before choosing your fabrics. Look for fabric with different tones – that is, areas of dark and light. You will then be able to use your pattern window to give the apples form – they will appear rounded instead of flat. Good enough to pick!

Technique used

∽ Pattern windows

FINISHED SIZE: 18½ x 14in (47 x 35.5cm)

The full-size templates and design for this project are on page 81

What you will need

∽ rectangles of three different background fabrics, each measuring 4½ x 9in

∽ appliqué fabrics:
   small pieces for the apples in colours of your choice
   small pieces of green for the leaves

∽ ⅛yd (10cm) sashing

∽ ½yd (40cm) fabric for the border and binding

∽ silk thread or alternative fine thread to match the appliqué fabrics

∽ freezer paper for the templates

∽ 20 x 16in low-loft wadding

∽ 20 x 16in backing fabric

Preparation

1 Cut each piece of background fabric in half to produce six background squares. Prepare each square

of background fabric by folding it and tacking the centre lines as described on page 11.

2 Trace the leaf template A on page 81 onto the matt side of the freezer paper; cut out the template carefully, leaving the background intact, to create a pattern window (see page 11). Move this over the fabric to view and select the best patterning on the fabric for the leaf. The photo detail above shows how you can use the fabric print to advantage to give shading and form to the apple shape.

TIP *Mark the tip of the leaf template and window with a dot - you won't then have the veins running in the wrong direction if you are using a directional print! (See page 11.)*

3 Place the template back in the hole and remove the window. (Note: the shiny side of the paper is placed against the right side of the fabric.) Use a hot iron to press the template to the fabric; cut out the shape, adding ⅛in seam allowance all around the shape.

Cut a total of six leaves in this way (**a**).

4 Repeat steps 2 and 3 with the apple template B on page 81 to prepare six apple shapes (**b**).

5 Using the full design on page 81 as a guide, position an apple and a leaf shape right side up on one of the background squares; pin the shapes in place, pinning in the seam allowance only. Work a few tacking stitches in the centre of the shape to secure it (see page 12).

6 Prepare the other squares in the same way.

Appliqué

1 Needle-turn all shapes in place; about 12-14 stitches to the inch will be adequate on these simple shapes. Make a small clip in the seam allowance on inner curves only, clipping only to half the depth of the seam allowance (see page 14).

Once you have completed a shape, peel off the template (**c**); the templates can be reused many times, so store them in a labelled envelope for future use!

2 Complete the appliqué on each of the six squares. Once the squares are finished, lay them right side down on a well-padded surface and press the back of the work.

Assembling the quilt

1 From the sashing fabric, cut:
  four strips each measuring 1¼ x 4½in (these are your A strips)
  three strips each measuring 1¼ x 14in (B strips)
  two strips each measuring 1¼ x 10¾in (C strips)

From the border fabric, cut:
  two strips each measuring 2¼ x 15½in (D strips)
  two strips each measuring 2¼ x 14¼in (E strips)

2 Assemble the quilt as shown, taking ¼in seams. Seam a sashing strip A to the lower edge of blocks 1, 2, 3 and 4 (**d**); press all the seams to one side, away from the blocks,

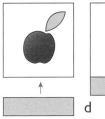

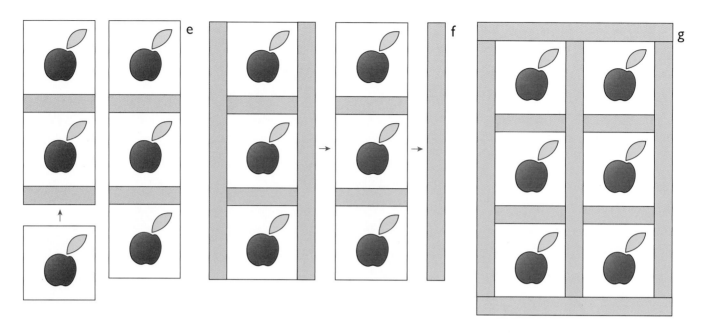

then join the six blocks into two strips of three blocks (**e**). Add sashing strips B as shown (**f**). Finally, add sashing strips C to the top and bottom of the design (**g**). Add the border strips, adding the D strips first and then the E strips (**h**). Remember to press each seam as it is completed.

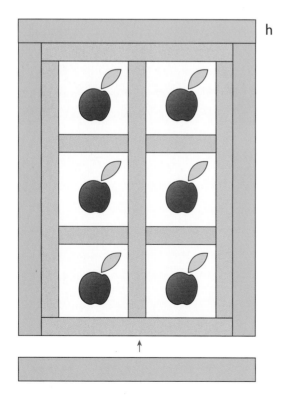

3 Layer the apple design with the wadding and backing (see page 74) to prepare it for quilting.

Quilting

Although I quilted the original by hand, you could use machine quilting instead.

1 If you would like to hand quilt, stitch around the leaves and apples about ⅛in outside the appliqué. This helps to bring the appliqué shapes 'forward' from the background and gives a raised effect.

2 There are many ways in which you could choose to quilt the background. In the original I used echo quilting, following the outlines of the apples and leaves and increasing the spacing between the 'echoes' as the quilting neared the border.

Finishing

1 Trim the quilt to an accurate rectangle and tack the raw edges together with a small running stitch.

2 Cut straight binding strips 1⅛in wide, and use these to bind the edges of the quilt (see page 75).

3 Attach a hanging sleeve to the back (see page 77).

Finally ...

Admire your first appliquéd quilt, and enjoy!

Project 3

Flower Faces Tote Bag

No cottage garden is complete without poppies; their cheerful, open faces of delicate petals brighten up the garden throughout the summer. Although today there is a wide range of poppy colours, the red ones seem to epitomise hot sunny days. The large flowering clematis is a more sophisticated addition to the garden with its showy blooms.

Both these flowers just seem perfect for appliqué and I have used them often in my designs; they both have interesting centres, so here is an opportunity to try two new techniques. I have used four little blocks and assembled them as part of a useful tote bag. You could use them in many different ways, perhaps as coasters, a notebook cover, greetings cards. Great for little gifts!

Techniques used

∞ flower centres

∞ overlapping shapes

FINISHED SIZE: approx 12 x 13½in (30 x 35cm)

The full-size templates for this project are on page 81

What you will need

∞ background fabric, four 4½in squares

∞ appliqué fabrics:
  red for the poppies
  purple for the clematis flowers
  two ¼ x 2in strips of gold
  scrap of olive green for the poppy centres

∞ fine thread to match the appliqué fabrics

∞ yellow, black and olive stranded embroidery floss

∞ Straw #11 needle for appliqué

∞ Crewel #6 needle for embroidery

∞ freezer paper for templates

∞ black Pigma™ 0.1 pen

∞ to make the bag
  ½yd (0.5m) main fabric
  ½yd (0.5m) lining fabric
  32 x 18in low-loft wadding
  ½yd (0.5m) lightweight backing fabric for quilting

Preparation

1 Trace the poppy template (A) on page 81 onto freezer paper, and cut out the shape leaving a pattern window (see page 11). Use the pattern window to select the print area for the poppy. Try to use a shaded print that suggests the 'breaks' in the petals, especially at the deeper indentations on the outer edge; you will find the window very useful for helping you to choose just the right area of shading. Iron the template in place and cut out the shape, adding the seam allowance all round.

2 Trace the clematis templates (D and E) onto freezer paper and cut them out, leaving a pattern window. Mark the dotted lines on template D. Use pattern windows as before and cut out the two shapes in fabric.

Appliqué

Poppy

1 Position the poppy centrally on one of the background squares, and appliqué the outer edge of the poppy in your chosen method (**a**).

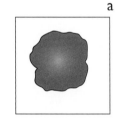
a

2 Use template B on page 81 to cut a 1in circle of olive green fabric for the poppy centre. Use template C on page 81 to cut a ½in circle in card, or use a pre-cut Mylar™ plastic circle. Use the fabric over the card or plastic shape to make a perfect circle (see page 17); remove the card or plastic shape. Pin the fabric circle in the centre of the poppy; using three strands of embroidery floss, work a wheel of blanket stitches to attach the flower centre to the poppy (**b**).

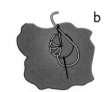
b

3 Use one strand of black and one of olive embroidery floss together to work French knots around the flower centre (**c**).

c

4 With the permanent marking pen, ink in additional shading (**d**).

d

g

Clematis

1 Position shape D centrally on a background square and appliqué it in position. Note that the edges marked with a dotted line are not turned under; leave these raw and secure them onto the background with a few running stitches (**e**).

e

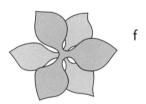

f

2 Appliqué shape E, using diagram **f** as a placement guide.

3 On one of the gold centre strips, work a small running stitch along one long raw edge; pull the thread up tightly to form a circle. Fray the outer edge and sew the circle into the centre of the clematis. Using two strands of yellow embroidery floss work a few French knots in the centre of the flower (**g**).

Make two clematis blocks and two poppy blocks. Press the work from the back on a padded surface.

Finishing

(¼in seam allowances are included in the measurements)

From the main fabric cut:
  one 13¼ x 15in piece for the bag back
  two 18 x 2¾in strips for the handles
  two 4½ x 1¼in strips (strips A and B)
  two 9¼ x 1¼in strips (C and D)

one 9¼ x 2½in strip (G)
two 13 x 2½in strips (H and I)
one 13¼ x 2½in strip (J)

From the red appliqué fabric cut: one 9¼ x 1in strip (E)

From the purple appliqué fabric cut: one 9¼ x 1in strip (F)

From the lining fabric cut: two 13¼ x 14½in pieces

From the backing fabric cut:
  two 15 x 17in pieces for the quilted bag front and back

From the wadding cut:
  two 15 x 17in pieces for the quilted bag front and back
  two 1 x 18in pieces for the bag handles.

1 Follow the sequence shown in the diagrams (**h-j**) to assemble the bag front, stitching by machine and taking ¼in seams throughout. As you work, press the seams away from the appliqué blocks each time; make sure that you press each seam before crossing it with another.

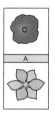

h

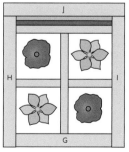

i

j

2 Layer the bag front with wadding and backing fabric to make a quilt sandwich (see page 74); secure the layers with safety pins as you will be machine-quilting the design.

3 Quilt 'in the ditch' along the seam lines as shown in diagram **k**, or use your own chosen quilting design.

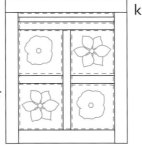

k

4 Layer the bag back as in step 2; quilt using the pattern of your choice, working to within 1in of the fabric edge. On the original I did very open stipple stitching. (Dense quilting will stiffen the fabric as well as shrinking it quite a bit.) Work a line of stitching all the way round the quilted bag back, 1in from the edge.

5 Trim the back and front pieces to 13¼ x 15in.

6 Now it's time to make the handles. On one long edge of each handle strip, press under ¼in to the wrong side.

Position one of the long strips of wadding centrally on the wrong side of the handle strip (**l**); fold over the raw edge, then fold over the opposite edge to overlap the raw edge. Machine down the centre of the handle close to the folded edge (**m**). Make another handle in the same way.

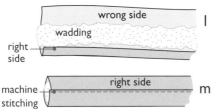

wrong side
wadding
right side
l
right side
machine stitching
m

7 With the right sides together, pin the handles in position on the bag front (**n**). Pin the handles to the bag back in the same way.

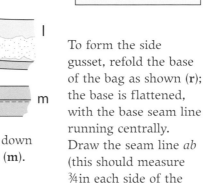

4in
n

8 Place the bag front and one lining piece right sides together, sandwiching the handles between the two layers. Machine a ¼in seam along the top edge of the bag (**o**). Repeat with the bag back and the remaining piece of lining. Note that the lining is shorter than the main bag – there is a reason for this!

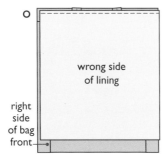

o
wrong side of lining
right side of bag front

9 Open out the bag front and lining (**p**). Open out the bag back and lining and pin this piece, right sides together, to the bag front; take care to match the seams joining the lining to the bag. Machine all the way around, leaving a 4in gap in the lining (**q**). (As my lining was red, I changed the thread colour to match; you could also line the bag with yellow, though, as shown in the diagrams, or in blue.)

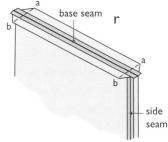

p

wrong side of bag front

wrong side of lining front

4in

q

To form the side gusset, refold the base of the bag as shown (**r**); the base is flattened, with the base seam line running centrally. Draw the seam line *ab* (this should measure ¾in each side of the base seam line); machine the marked seam.

a
base seam
r
b
a
b
side seam

10 Turn the bag to the right side through the gap in the lining, then sew up the gap.

11 Push the lining down inside the bag (the top of the bag folds down inside for ¾in; this creates a neater edge). Stitch the handles firmly to the inside of the top edge of the bag (**s**).

12 You can top-stitch around the top of the bag if you wish, but I preferred to hand-sew in the ditch between the lining and the bag, taking the stitch only into the wadding so it is not visible on the outside of the bag.

Your bag is now complete. The integral gusset makes it a roomy, useful bag. You could stitch on a popper closure for greater security, add pockets to the inner lining, or even put a pocket on the back. Personalise it to meet your needs!

s
handles stitched to inside edge

⤳ *Project 4* ⤳

Cyclamen Glasses Case

Small cyclamen create a beautiful carpet under leafless trees. This stitched version is a simple design that is just right for a glasses case which can be hung round the neck. (I find this kind of case very useful, as I am always mislaying my specs!) It would also make a safe storage case for your rotary cutter or scissors. It is very easy to change the dimensions to make similar containers for various other items.

You can see how I have used the fabric print to advantage to create shading on the petals and leaves. Try to find a patterned fabric which will suggest the distinctive markings of cyclamen leaves - that is not easy, but is a good excuse for browsing in the quilt shops ...

Techniques used

 ∾ fine stems
 ∾ overlay for appliqué placement
 ∾ unit appliqué

FINISHED SIZE: approx 6½ x 3½in (16.5cm x 8.5cm)

The full-size templates and design for this project are on page 83

What you will need

 ∾ 4 x 14in outer fabric
 ∾ 4 x 14in lining fabric
 ∾ 4 x 14in low-loft wadding
 ∾ appliqué fabrics:
   small piece of green for the leaves.
   small piece for the cyclamen in your colour of choice (cyclamen come in a many colours – if you choose a pale colour consider having a dark background fabric)
   small piece of pink for the stem
 ∾ fine thread to match the appliqué fabrics
 ∾ pink and yellow stranded embroidery floss
 ∾ Straw #11 needle for the appliqué
 ∾ 4 x 6½in lightweight interfacing for the overlay
 ∾ freezer paper for templates
 ∾ 1yd (1m) hand-made or purchased cord

Preparation

1 Fold the background fabric in half lengthways and finger-press the fold; tack along this line to mark the centre line. Tack a line across the fabric 3in from the end. These lines help centre the design on the front of the glasses case.

2 Place the fabric over the design, matching the tacked centre lines with the centre lines on the design. (You may find it easier to do this using a traced or photocopied version of the design rather than laying the fabric directly on the book.) Use masking tape in the corners to hold both the design and the fabric in position while you trace. Trace the solid stem lines only onto the fabric – you could make the stem in one piece (see diagram **c**). If your background is dark use a white pencil. This is the only part which will be marked on the fabric; you will position everything else with the aid of the overlay.

 ∾ **TIP** *Use a light-box (or tape the design to a window) to trace the stem positions if you cannot see the design through your chosen fabric.*

Overlay

1 Trace the design onto the interfacing, following the instructions on page 18 to make the overlay.

2 Position the overlay on the background so that the centre lines match. Pin the ends of the centre lines, then tack the overlay securely in position

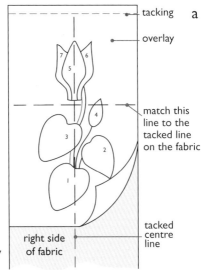

along the top edge of the background fabric (**a**). Remove the pins, and roll up the overlay when it is not in use.

Appliqué

Main stem

The fine stem method is used to make the main stem. This is a useful stem technique which can successfully be used to stitch stems varying from ¼-⅛in finished width. Obviously stems feature in a lot of flower designs, so it is a useful technique to learn early on.

1 Cut a 3in bias strip from stem fabric, ¾in wide. The easiest way to do this is using a rotary cutter on a cutting mat; if you do not have rotary-cutting equipment you can use a strip of ¾in masking tape as a guide (**b**); place the tape on the bias of the fabric and cut up each side.

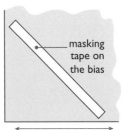

 ∾ **TIP** *It's important to cut all stems on the bias so that they will mould to curves and sit smoothly on the background.*

2 Fold the strip in half, wrong sides together, and finger-press along its length.

3 Place the cut edges against the marked stem line with the cut edges to the right and the folded edge on the left. Note that the stem has to extend ⅛in under the leaf and flower. However, as the right-hand side of the stem is longer at the top than the left-hand side – because of the shape of the flower – you will need to ensure that a more generous amount of stem is left under the flower. You can always trim off the excess

later if you have too much stem left when you stitch the flower in place. Pin the stem, placing the pins at right angles to the edge (**c**).

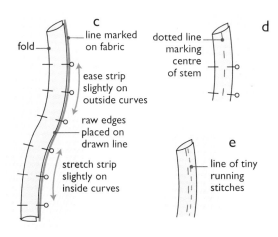

4 Mark the centre of the strip with a few dots (**d**).

5 Stitch the stem with a small running stitch just above the dots, nearer the cut edge (**e**). There is a reason for not stitching exactly along the centre. You need a thread or two of fabric to allow for the take-up on the curve when the folded edge is turned over the raw edge at the next stage; if you stitch exactly in the centre you will find that the strip will not cover the drawn line. So work the running stitch slightly off-centre and you will not have this problem.

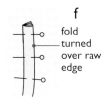

6 Fold the folded edge over the raw edges and pin it at right angles (**f**); appliqué the folded edge in place (**g**).

Leaves

1 Trace each numbered shape #1-#3 onto the matt side of the freezer paper.

2 Cut out each shape carefully, leaving pattern windows which can be passed over the appliqué fabric to select the most effective part of the fabric print to use. For example, try to find an area to suggest the markings on the leaves. When you have found the ideal placement, drop the template back in the hole, remove the pattern window, and iron the template in place. (Remember that this is all done on the *right* side of the fabric.)

3 Cut out each shape adding a ⅛in seam allowance.

4 Use the overlay to position the leaves. Slide leaf #1 under the overlay and line it up with the design.

TIP *Use your turning stick or scissors point to manoeuvre the shape underneath the overlay.*

Pin and tack the shape in place (see page 12), then appliqué in place (see pages 13-16). Complete all the leaves in the same way.

Cyclamen

The flower-head introduces you to the technique of unit appliqué, which is a very useful method for pre-assembling units so that they can later be stitched onto the background. Note that the colour shading on the cyclamen is matched across all the petals (**h**).

1 Trace template #5 onto freezer paper; don't forget to copy the registration marks on the template. Cut out the shape, leaving a pattern window to select the fabric position. Iron the template in place and cut out, adding seam allowance (see steps 1-3 under *Leaves*). Draw round the template with white marking pen; also mark the registration marks in the seam allowance (**i**). Remove the template.

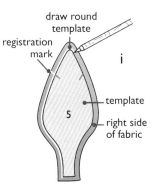

2 Pin prepared shape #5 to a piece of the cyclamen fabric (**j**).

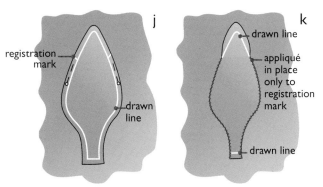

Stitch in place from the registration mark to the base on each side of petal #5; leave the lower edge raw (**k**).

3 Iron in place templates #6 and #7 each side of #5; check for accuracy with the overlay and adjust the pieces if necessary. Cut out the complete cyclamen (**l**). Draw round the outer edges of templates #6 and #7. Keep the freezer paper in place; this will help you position the cyclamen on the background, and can be removed once the flower is pinned in position on the background fabric.

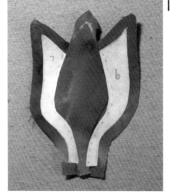

4 On the reverse, cut away the surplus fabric under #5 (**m**). The advantage of this method is that you can closely trim the seam allowances and get a smooth, flat finish. Press from the back.

m

5 Appliqué the whole unit in place, using the overlay as a positioning guide. Clip the inner curves to give a smooth line.

6 Finally appliqué the bud in position.

Embellishing

Embroidery

Embroider the remaining stems using two strands of pink stranded embroidery floss and a small stem stitch.

Work a few straight stitches in yellow at the base of the cyclamen flower (see close-up **h** on page 33).

Quilting

The back of the glasses case is quilted with a cyclamen outline (**n**).

1 Lightly trace the whole of the design onto the fabric – check the position carefully, and ensure that the cyclamen faces the cut end!

2 Pin the wadding behind the marked fabric. Machine or hand quilt the outline cyclamen on

n

the back of the case, using pink thread for the flower, bud and stems; change to green for the leaves.

3 Machine or hand quilt around the appliquéd cyclamen design, and quilt a centre vein on the leaves.

Finishing

1 Pin the appliqué and the lining right sides together.

2 Stitch a ¼in seam across each short end (**o**).

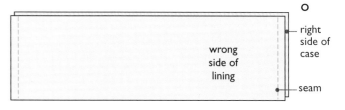

o

right side of case

wrong side of lining

seam

3 Re-position the two fabrics as shown in diagram **p**. Stitch ¼in side seams, leaving a gap as shown for turning.

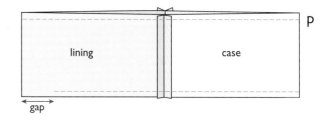

p

lining

case

gap

4 Turn the case right side out, and close the gap in the lining by machine or hand. Push the lining down inside the case.

5 Stitch the cord securely to the top of the case.

Flowers with Dimension

Dimensional techniques are my favourites: I love to experiment and create dimensional flowers to add texture and further visual interest to my hand appliqué designs.

When I first saw an original 1840s Baltimore Album Quilt I was struck by the amount of dimensional work; some of the roses were highly padded, and ruching techniques abounded. These Victorian quilters were very inventive, and their work serves as inspiration for us today; nowadays we also have the added advantage of beautiful batiks and a vast array of other fabrics to use in our

appliqué. Many of the blocks and quilts in this book incorporate dimensional flowers, buds and fruit. To get you started, I'll begin with some very easy flowers which can be made from Suffolk Puffs (known as Yo-Yos in the US).

As dimensional flowers are usually pleated or gathered in some way it is best to use the lighter-weight cotton fabrics which can be gathered neatly. Silk fabrics make beautiful flowers, but as they tend to fray it's best to practise with cotton for your first attempts!

Suffolk Puff flowers

Suffolk Puffs are very simple to make and can be adapted to create several styles of flowers. They may not be botanically correct, but if you use the appropriate fabric colour and scale, your flower will 'read' as a violet, forget-me-not or buttercup etc. These little flowers make great 'fillers' in a design; they also look delightful on fabric box-tops, and can make very pretty cards.

Basic method

1 Use template A on page 99 to draw a 2in diameter circle on fabric; cut it out on the drawn line.

2 Use regular sewing thread in a matching colour to work small running stitches close to the outer edge (**a**). (On the diagrams I've used a contrasting colour so that you can see what's happening.)

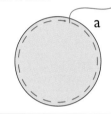

∾ **TIP** *Fasten the thread on securely at the start of your stitching line, as you will be pulling it up to gather the fabric.*

---

3 Pull up the gathers tightly, and fasten off the thread but do not cut it. Flatten the shape as shown (**b**).

4 Bring the needle up in the centre on the 'smooth' side of the Suffolk Puff and make a small stitch in the centre. Take the needle to the edge of the puff and catch a thread (**c**). Pass the needle into the centre at the back and through to the right side (**d**).

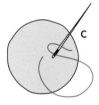

Place your thumb over the stitch and pull it up tightly (**e**). Catching the outer edge as you make this stitch keeps the stitch in position, which is useful when you make the rest of the stitches to divide the shape into evenly-sized petals. To keep the tension tight it's a good idea to make a second stitch in the same place (without catching the edge this time, of course).

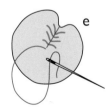

5 To divide the puff into three petals, make two more dividing wraps in the same way (**f**), and fasten off the thread. Work a French knot in the centre – or perhaps sew on a small bead.

Depending on your choice of colour you will now have made either a violet, a forget-me-not or a small blossom (**g**)! There are lots of possibilities.

You can change the size of the circle and divide it into three, four or five petals (**h**). Five petals are a bit more challenging to get even-sized – but then are all the petals evenly-sized on a flower?

Getting smaller!

If you use a ¾in circle you can make super little flowers, but taking the necessary very small seam allowance can be tricky.

Here is a tip from my quilting friend, Nancy Kerns. Draw the circle on the fabric but work the gathering on the drawn line *before* cutting out the circle (**i**).

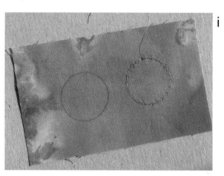

You can then cut very close to the stitching and have a very tiny seam allowance with little bulk; this is important when working on such a small scale (**j**, enlarged detail). These tiny flowers can be divided in the same way as the larger ones into three, four or five petals.

Examples of these small flowers can be seen in the *Blue Vase* quilt (see page 39) and in *Summer Bounty* (see page 62).

✣ *Variations* ✣

Try stitching a small three-petalled flower to the centre of a larger one to give a two-tiered flower.

1 Cut a 1⅛in circle and make a Suffolk Puff as described earlier, but do not completely close the centre when you are pulling up the gathers (**a**). (This creates a little hollow to accommodate the smaller Suffolk Puff which you will later place on top.) Divide the puff into three petals (**b**).

2 Cut a 1in circle and make a smaller Suffolk Puff; pull up the gathers tightly and divide the shape into three petals (**c**).

3 Lay the larger puff raw edge uppermost, then position the smaller puff on top with the raw edge underneath. Stitch the smaller puff in place, and add French knots in the centre (**d**).

Another way of varying this technique is to make a hemmed Suffolk Puff, by turning a ⅛in hem to the wrong side as you work the gathering close to the folded edge (**e**). Because of the bulk of the hem you will not be able to close the centre hole completely when you pull up the gathers, but you can push in a little contrast scrap of fabric to fill the centre (**f**).

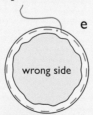
wrong side

Still another idea is to pull up the Suffolk Puff to make a 'cup' shape which can be stuffed. Cut a circle of contrast fabric about the same size as the original circle used for the puff. Work a running stitch around the edge, pull the shape up slightly and fill it with stuffing; push the stuffed puff inside the hemmed puff (**g**).

You can also divide a hemmed puff into three petals and maybe embroider French knots in the centre (**h**).

The hemmed version is also useful for daffodil trumpets. Pull the gathers up only partially to make a 'cup' shape. If you wish, you can pull the trumpet up round a piece of dowel, then paint it with spray starch and leave it to dry (**i**).

This idea works well for purely decorative projects. On more functional projects I use a hemmed Suffolk Puff pulled up partially and used as a flat centre (**j**).

Small hemmed puffs also make excellent dimensional flower centres (see *Summer Bounty* on page 63).

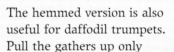

~ Project 5 ~

A Posy of Violets

Here is a quick project using dimensional flowers: a posy of fabric violets makes a pretty card for someone special. The flowers and leaves are glued in position; add a narrow ribbon bow for a finishing touch.

Technique used

~ Suffolk Puff flowers

The full-size templates for this project are on page 99

What you will need

~ blank greetings card

~ fabrics:
    scrap of lightweight purple cotton for the flowers
    scrap of green for the leaves

~ regular sewing thread to match the flower fabric

~ yellow stranded embroidery floss

~ iron-on interfacing

~ 9in very narrow ribbon

~ fabric glue

~ black or brown fineliner

Making the posy

Flowers

Use template B and make three Suffolk Puffs using the basic method described on page 36. Divide each flower into three or four petals. Using two strands of the embroidery floss, embroider a French knot in the centre of each flower – or you could add a bead in the centre of each flower if you prefer.

Leaves

Iron the interfacing onto the wrong side of the leaf fabric, and use the leaf template to cut out the leaves. I 'fussy-cut' my leaves from a leaf print fabric – that is, using a pattern window to isolate a particular area of the print for each appliqué shape; if you prefer, you could use a plain fabric and ink in vein lines with a fine permanent pen.

You could make different-shaped leaves to go with your chosen flower, but keep it simple!

Assembly

Using the glue sparingly, stick the leaves and flowers in position on the card front. Make a bow with the ribbon and glue it in position; keep the loops and ends free for a dimensional look. Ink in a few stems, and your posy is complete.

Send the card to someone special who will appreciate your efforts!

Blue Vase

This small wall quilt includes a number of dimensional flower techniques. You will recognise the small Suffolk Puff flowers used for the tiny violets and the orange flower centres. The orange flowers themselves are made from a ruched strip of fabric; the larger purple flower is also made from a ruched strip. Another version of a Suffolk Puff is used for the lily of the valley; simple appliquéd leaves and a blue vase complete the design.

Techniques used

∾ ruched flowers

∾ variations of Suffolk Puffs

∾ attachment of dimensional flowers

FINISHED SIZE: 11¼ x 13¾in
(28.5 x 35cm)

The full-size templates and design for this project are on page 82

What you will need

∾ 8 x 10½in background fabric

∾ appliqué fabrics:
   5 x 4in piece for the vase
   small piece of green for the leaves
   three 1⅛ x 5½in strips for the orange flowers (cut on the straight grain)
   one 1⅛ x 15in strip for the purple flower (cut on the straight grain)
   small pieces in purple for the violets and pink for the lilies of the valley

∾ 8 x 6in lightweight interfacing for the overlay

∾ silk thread or alternative fine thread to match the appliqué fabrics

∾ regular sewing thread to match the flowers

- yellow and green stranded embroidery floss
- for quilting the design:
  - 12 x 15in low-loft wadding
  - 12 x 15in backing fabric
- fabrics for the borders and binding:
  - 4 x 11in for the inner border
  - 12 x 10in for the outer border
  - 1⅛ x 56in binding
- fine permanent marking pen

Preparation

1 Fold the background fabric lengthways and finger-press the centre. Tack along this crease to mark the centre line.

2 Follow the instructions on page 18 to make an overlay from the design.

3 Position the overlay on the background, matching the centre lines and placing the base of the vase 1¾in from the lower edge of the fabric. Tack securely along the top edge (**a**).

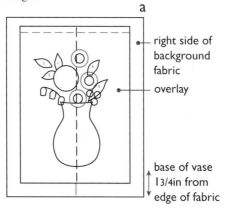

- right side of background fabric
- overlay
- base of vase 13/4in from edge of fabric

Creating the design

Appliqué

1 Trace the templates for the pot and the leaves (#1-5) onto the matt side of the freezer paper. Cut out these shapes to produce pattern windows (see page 11), then use the pattern windows to select and prepare the shapes for appliqué. Use the overlay to help you position the leaf shapes and the pot on the background, then appliqué them in place (see pages 13-17).

2 Press the completed appliqué from the back.

Dimensional flowers

Small ruched flowers

1 Working with one strip of orange fabric, press one long edge under (to the wrong side of the fabric) by ⅜in, then press the opposite edge under by ¼in. (Note that these turnings will overlap slightly on the back of the strip.) Position the folded strip on the guide (**b**),

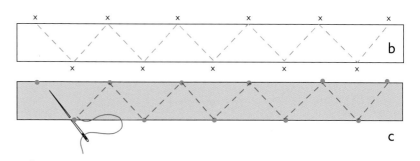

and lightly mark the X points on each fold. Using matching sewing thread, work small running stitches as shown on the guide (**c**). Remember to fasten on securely, as you will be pulling up the thread!

- **TIP** *At each point marked X, make the stitch over the folded edge. This helps to create more defined petal shapes when the strip is gathered.*

2 Pull up the strip until it measures 3in and fasten off the thread; distribute the gathers evenly along the strip.

3 You will now have a ruched strip as shown (**d**). Examine your strip carefully. You should have five complete petals on one side of the strip; the opposite edge will have four complete petals and also two half-petals – one at each end of the strip. This is the side you need to draw up to make the flower. Secure the thread at point Y and catch the petal bases, including the two halves as shown (**e**). Pull the thread up tightly and secure it.

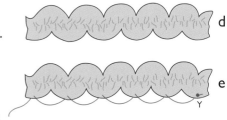

4 Neatly seam the two ends, pulling tightly between the petals at the outer edge to produce a neat shape (**f**). If the seam is too bulky, trim it at this stage.

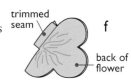

trimmed seam

back of flower

5 There are various ways in which you can make the centre of the flower. You could add beads or French knots. In this example I made a basic Suffolk Puff. If you would like to do the same, cut a 1in circle (template C) and work a running stitch close to the edge (**g**). Pull it up tightly, then flatten it (**h**), and work French knots in centre. Sew it in the centre of the flower (**i**). Make all three orange flowers in the same way.

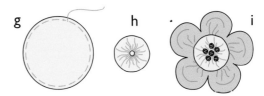

Large ruched flower

1 Mark and gather the strip as described above for the orange flowers; keep moving the strip over the guide to mark the complete length.

2 Draw up the first petals as for the small flower, but do not make the seam.

3 Tuck under the start of the strip and coil the extra length of the ruched strip behind the centre to make a second circuit of petals. With small stitches, catch the petal tips from the first round to the centre of the second round (**j**). Tuck in the end of the strip behind the second circuit of petals to neaten it off.

Small violets

1 Trace round template D (¾in circle) onto the fabric. Work a small running stitch on the marked line; do not fasten off the thread.

2 Cut out the circle leaving a very small seam allowance (see 'Getting smaller!' on page 36). Pull up the gathers tightly. Work stitches over the edge from the centre to divide the circle into three petals (see page 36).

3 Embroider a French knot in the centre of the flower. Make each violet in the same way.

Lily of the valley

1 Trace template C (1in circle) onto the fabric and cut out the circle along the marked edge. Work a running stitch just inside the edge, but do not fasten off the thread (**k**).

2 Pull the shape up partially, fold it in half, and flatten it to produce a bell shape. Fasten off the thread. Ruffle the raw edge slightly (**l**).

k

fold shape **l**
in half

pull up
gathers

ruffle edge

Sewing on the dimensional flowers

1 Pin the flowers in position on the background as shown on the design (**m**).

2 Stitch each flower in place with running stitches, working from the back; you will be able to feel the outline of the flower underneath.

m

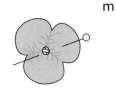

Stitch just inside the outer edge of the shape, catching only the back layer of the flower (**n**); this way the flowers will maintain their dimensional appearance. It is also much easier to sew on bulky features this way than trying to sew round the edge on the front of the work.

wrong side

Embroidery

Embroider the stems for the lily of the valley and the leaf; work in stem stitch using two strands of green embroidery floss.

Finishing

Borders

1 From the inner border fabric cut:

two 1 x 10½in strips for the side borders

two 1 x 8in strips for the top and bottom borders

From the outer border fabric cut:

two 2¼ x 10½in strips for the side borders

two 2¼ x 11½in strips for the top and bottom borders

2 Follow the instructions on pages 73-74 to add first the inner and then the outer borders.

Quilting

1 Follow the instructions on page 74 to layer the appliqué, the wadding and the backing fabric.

2 Hand quilt a scant ⅛in around the edge of the appliqué design.

3 For the background quilting, you can choose your own design. I went slightly mad on mine and did lots of echo quilting; I also used the leaf templates to trace a few extra leaf shapes on the background, and integrated these into the echo quilting. The borders were random quilted following the fabric print. I could get away with less quilting on the border of this small quilt, but on a larger piece I'm sure I would have ended up with a wavy edge to the quilt; to prevent this happening, it's advisable to keep the density of the quilting even across the surface of the quilt.

Binding

Trim the quilt to an accurate rectangle, then follow the instructions on page 75 to bind the edges of the quilt.

❧ *Variations* ❧

This is another version of the *Blue Vase* design. On this one I have replaced the orange ruched flowers with another style of dimensional flower; these are a little trickier to make, but I'm sure you can rise to the challenge!

Folded five-petalled flower (a).

1 Cut a 1in diameter circle for the centre; follow the instructions on page 36 to make this into a Suffolk Puff.

2 Stitch the centre in position on the background, securing it in the centre only (**b**); leave the outer edge free so that you can slide the petals underneath.

3 Cut five circles, each 1¼in in diameter, for the petals. Fold each circle into quarters as shown (**c**), and gather the lower edge with a small running stitch (**d**); pull up the gathers tightly (**e**).

a

b

c · d · e

right side

4 Arrange the petals around the flower centre, overlapping them slightly and tucking in the raw edges so that they are covered by the centre. Pin each petal in place (**f**).

5 Stab stitch around the flower centre to secure the petals; be careful to keep all the raw edges tucked under the centre (**g**).

f

g

❧ **TIP** *To help you keep the petals in an accurate circle, use a circle template (the 1⅛in size is about right). Place the template over the flower; it's then much easier to arrange the petals evenly in the circular aperture (**h**).*

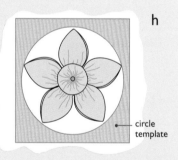

h

circle template

6 Embroider a few French knots in the centre of the flower – this helps to secure the raw edges.

Further possibilities

A folded petal also makes a pretty bud; cover the raw edges with an appliquéd calyx.

Appliqué Blocks and Quilts

∾ *Project 7* ∾

Hydrangeas

Hydrangea flowers change colour according to their age and the soil conditions in which they are growing. Their delicate colouring, shading through pink, blue and pale green, inspired this design. I prefer the paler, more faded colourings rather than the hot pinks, and I was fortunate to find a batik fabric which included all these colours.

The flowers are complemented by the large copper pot which was fussy-cut (see page 6) from a batik fabric; you can see the way in which I have used the fabric shading which gives form to the pot. This may look like a complicated design, but it's actually very easy, and uses techniques which have already been covered earlier in the book. The simple leaves are not difficult to needle-turn, and the flowers are made from Suffolk Puffs.

The very soft, subtle background shading works well with the colours of the flowers. A narrow border of the hydrangea fabric continues the theme before the final border is added. You could combine this block with others in this book, or border it as shown here to make a wall quilt or cushion.

Techniques used

∾ overlay for appliqué placement

∾ Suffolk Puffs

∾ overlapping shapes

FINISHED SIZE: the centre block is approximately 11½in (29cm) square

The full-size templates and design for this project are on pages 83-85

What you will need

∾ 11½in square background fabric (or larger if you prefer)

∾ appliqué fabrics:
  equivalent of ¼yd for the flowers
  small piece of green for the leaves
  6in square for the pot

∾ fine thread to match the appliqué fabrics

∾ regular sewing thread to tone with the flower fabric

- yellow stranded embroidery floss
- Straw #11 needle for appliqué
- Crewel #6 needle for embroidery
- 11in square lightweight interfacing for the overlay
- freezer paper for templates
- If you would like to border the block as shown in the photograph you will need the following:
  four 1 x 11½in strips for the inner border
  two 2½ x 11½in strips for the outer border
  two 2½ x 15½in strips for the outer border

Preparation

1 Fold the background fabric and tack the centre lines as described on page 11.

2 Trace the two sections of the full-size design onto paper, carefully matching the centre lines to create the complete design.

3 Follow the instructions on page 18 to make the overlay and attach it to the background, matching the centre lines.

Appliqué

Pot

1 Trace the pot (template #1) onto freezer paper. Normally you would trace templates from the design, but in this instance you need to needle-turn the edges which are hidden by the flowers. (Usually when this happens the edge is left as a raw edge and not turned under; simply use a small running stitch to hold the edge in place. In this design, though, there may be gaps between the flowers so the edge will not be totally covered, so it's better to needle-turn it; that's why I have provided a separate template.) Once you have traced the shape onto the freezer paper, cut it out, leaving a pattern window (see page 11).

2 Use the pattern window to select the print area for the pot. Consider the direction the light is falling across your design, and try to be consistent where you use the light and dark shadings on the fabric. The pattern windows are very helpful in this respect. I usually mark the pattern window and template to indicate the light and dark sides of the shape, otherwise it can get a bit confusing!

3 Appliqué the pot in place (**a**). Note that the edges covered by leaves #15 and #16 are not needle-turned; leave them as raw edges, and simply secure them in place with a small running stitch (**b**).

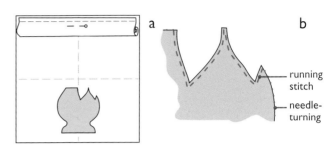

Leaves

1 Trace each numbered shape #2-#16 onto the matt side of the freezer paper. Cut out the templates to leave pattern windows, and use these to position the leaf templates on the fabric. Remember the light direction!

2 Cut out the leaves and appliqué them in place.

3 Press the appliqué from the back before stitching on the flowers.

Flowers

1 Make the flowers using the Suffolk Puff technique (see page 36) and a 1½in circle of fabric. You will need approximately 56! This is a useful take-along piece of stitching for when you are travelling, visiting or waiting for an appointment. Vary the colouring for a natural look. You can also make some smaller flowers if you like, for fillers, using a 1¼in circle.

2 Divide each flower into four petals, and embroider a French knot in the centre of each flower.

3 Arrange the flowers on the background (**c**) using the dotted line on the overlay as a guide. Pin them in place and sew them on from the back (see page 41).

Finishing

Borders

1 Trim the block to an accurate 11½in square (see page 72). Follow the instructions on pages 73-74 to add first the inner borders and then the outer borders.

❧ *Project 8* ❧

Autumn Glory

There is a young oak tree slowly growing at the bottom of my garden and it will be there for future generations to see in its full maturity! In the language of flowers, acorns symbolise longevity. They seem very appropriate in this autumnal quilt; I hope our quilts will provide pleasure for future generations. For most of the oak leaves and border triangles I used a beautiful African fabric; I didn't really want to cut into it but it seemed perfect for this project.

In this project you will be able to practise making perfect circles for the berries as well as needle-turning lots of curves and points. The unusual setting of the block makes an interesting frame for a one-block quilt.

The Appliqué Garden

Technique used

∿ Perfect circles

FINISHED SIZE: the appliqué design measures approx 12in (30cm) square. The finished quilt measures 21½in (54cm) square

The full-size templates and design for this project are on pages 86-91

What you will need

∿ 16in square background fabric

∿ appliqué fabric
  small pieces in a range of autumnal colours of your choice for the stems and leaves
  red/orange for berries and fungi
  light brown for fungi stems
  a different light brown for the acorns

∿ ¼yd (0.2m) for the border triangles

∿ ⅜yd (0.3m) for the outer border

∿ ¼yd (0.2m) for binding

∿ fine threads to match the appliqué fabrics

∿ light and medium brown stranded embroidery floss

∿ Straw #11 needle for appliqué

∿ Crewel #6 needle for embroidery

∿ 14in square lightweight interfacing for the overlay

∿ freezer paper for templates

∿ black Pigma™ pen 0.1

∿ to complete the quilt:
  24in square low-loft wadding
  24in square backing fabric

Preparation

1 Fold the background fabric and tack the centre lines as described on page 11.

2 Trace the four sections of the full-size design onto paper, carefully matching the centre lines to create the complete design.

3 Trace through the solid lines of the stems onto the fabric. (This is the only part of the design which is marked on the fabric; you will position the rest of the appliqué with the aid of the overlay.) When you are tracing onto the fabric, remember to tape the design to the work surface first.

Then tape the fabric on top, ensuring that the centre lines of the design match up with the centre lines tacked on the fabric.

4 Follow the instructions on page 18 to make the overlay and attach it to the background, matching the centre lines.

Appliqué

Stems

1 Cut ¾in bias strips for the stems (note that the ends of the stems extend for ⅛in under the leaves).

2 Appliqué the stems using the fine stem method (see page 32). Remember to position the folded bias strip on the drawn line with the cut edges on the line and the folded edge facing inwards towards the centre of the block (**a**).

(You can also check with the overlay that the stem is correctly positioned.) Remember that on an outer curve the bias strip has to be eased slightly as

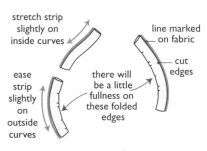

it is pinned in position, otherwise the background will pucker when the strip is folded over and stitched on the opposite edge. On an inner curve you need to stretch the strip slightly so that it lies smoothly when you stitch the second side of the stem.

Leaves, fungi and acorns

1 Appliqué these in number order using your chosen appliqué technique (**b**). Remember to clip the inner curves on the leaves (see page 14).

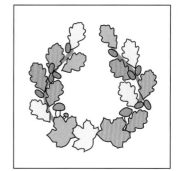

2 Embroider the acorn cups with French knots, using three strands of medium brown and one strand of light brown embroidery floss together.

∿ **TIP** *The embroidery is easier to work if you cut away some of the background fabric behind the acorns.*

Berries

1 Either accurately cut card circles, ½in and ⅜in in diameter, or use Mylar™ pre-cut circles (see page 17); the latter are heat resistant and more accurate.

2 Cut a 1in circle of fabric for each of the larger berries and use ⅞in circles for the small berries.

3 Prepare and appliqué the berries (**c**) using the perfect circles method (see page 17).

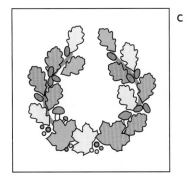

c

Pressing

Press the appliqué carefully from the back, placing the work face down on a well-padded surface.

Trim the background to an accurate 15in square (see page 72).

Finishing

Assembling the quilt top

1 Trace templates A-E onto the matt side of the freezer paper and cut them out. Carefully mark the points X, Y and Z where seams meet, and also mark the direction of the straight grain.

2 Using the fabric you have selected for the triangles, iron template A to the wrong side of the fabric. Draw round the template with pencil to mark the stitching line, then cut it out adding ¼in seam allowance; mark the matching points X, Y and Z. You will need to mark and cut eight fabric triangles in total.

3 Use the same technique to mark and cut two of each shape B, C, D and E from the outer border fabric. Mark the matching points X, Y and Z.

4 On the centre block mark points X and Y, 4½in from each corner (**d**). Position a triangle in each corner, right sides together and matching points X and Y (**e**).

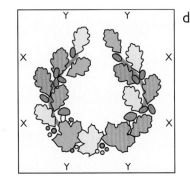

d

Machine a ¼in seam on each triangle, then press the seam towards the triangle. Check that the triangle is correctly positioned before trimming the background seam to ¼in (**f**).

5 Assemble the side borders by stitching B and C to A (**g**), matching points X, Y and Z carefully. Press the seams towards the triangles.

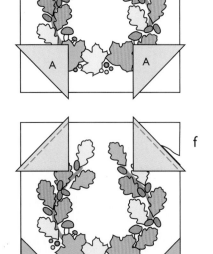

e

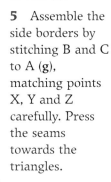

f

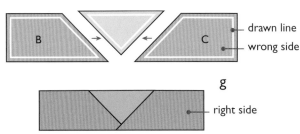

g

6 Stitch an assembled border unit to each side of the centre block (**h**). (Check that the triangles match on the edge of the centre block before machining.) Press the seams towards the border.

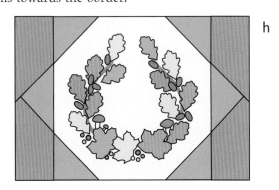

h

7 Assemble the top and bottom borders in a similar way using D and E on each side of A (**i**); stitch the top and bottom borders in place (**j**).

8 Press the quilt top on the reverse side.

The Appliqué Garden

i

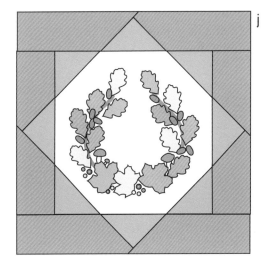

j

Quilting

1 Prepare the quilt sandwich (see page 74). Outline the appliqué design with hand quilting, stitching a very scant ⅛in from the edge, then quilt vein lines on the leaves.

2 On my original, I used a machine to work the rest of the quilting. However, it can be completely quilted by hand if you prefer; you could work rows of outline quilting about ½in apart around the appliqué on the background, and perhaps straight rows, 1in apart, diagonally in the borders.

3 If you would like to copy my ideas for machine quilting the background, start by stitching the outline oak leaves in the centre (**k**). Choose three of the freezer paper oak leaf templates you used for the appliqué, and lightly press them in position in the centre of appliqué so that you can use them as guides for the machine outline (or draw round each shape with a fine quilting pencil).

4 Once you have stitched the leaf outlines, stipple quilt the remainder of the centre background. Straight stitch around the octagon just inside the border.

5 Quilt the borders using the freezer paper leaf templates #14 and #15. Lightly press a leaf on each triangle and quilt round it; remove the paper shape and add vein lines on the leaf. Add further leaf shapes and quilt them in the same way to fill the border as shown on page 91 – you can use part leaves at the edges.

TIP *If you intend to machine quilt the top, use safety pins to keep the layers together. Tacking stitches will get trapped under the machining and you will then find it difficult to remove them.*

Binding

Trim the quilt to an accurate rectangle. Cut three binding strips, 2¼in wide, across the width of the fabric for the double binding. Follow the instructions on page 77 to bind the edges of the quilt.

k

～ Project 9 ～

Woodland Foxgloves

The bright, dramatic spires of foxgloves make lovely dimensional flowers. Although they are naturally woodland flowers, foxgloves have become a popular choice for cottage gardens, and they seed readily in my flower beds. Primroses and violets are also prolific and make a colourful carpet in the late spring; these little dimensional flowers are easy to make and add further interest to the design.

The twisted stems in this design introduce an alternative method for making stems. Why not try being a bit more adventurous in your choice of fabric for leaves? I used a beautiful purple/green leaf print to follow through the purple/pink shades used for the flowers, and quite a variety of other greens for the different types of leaves in this block. Once again, you could combine this block with others in the book or border it as a wall quilt.

Techniques used

- ∾ five-petalled Suffolk Puff flowers
- ∾ bias bar stems
- ∾ ruched flowers (see the variations on page 40)
- ∾ foxgloves

FINISHED SIZE: the appliqué design measures 10in (approx 25cm) square

The full-size templates and design for this project are on pages 91-93

What you will need

- ∾ 13in square background fabric (or larger if you prefer)
- ∾ appliqué fabric
  10in square bright pink for the foxgloves
  10in square pale pink for lining the foxgloves
  small pieces of a variety of greens for the leaves
  one 1 x 6in bias strip for the foxglove stems

The Appliqué Garden

one 1 x 24in (total length) bias strip for the twisted side stems (look for colour variations to produce tonal contrasts on the twisted stems) – you can use smaller lengths to make up the 24in total

small piece of purple for the violets

small piece of pale yellow for the primroses

- fine thread to match the appliqué fabrics
- regular sewing threads to tone with the flower fabrics
- yellow and green stranded embroidery floss
- Straw #11 needle for appliqué
- Crewel #6 needle for embroidery
- 11in square lightweight interfacing for the overlay
- freezer paper for templates
- ⅛in bias bar (a plastic electrical tie – the type used by electricians to tie together bundles of cables – works very well as an alternative; you will find these in DIY stores)

Preparation

1 Fold the background fabric and tack the centre lines as described on page 11.

2 Trace the two sections of the full-size design onto paper, carefully matching the centre lines to create the complete design.

3 To mark the stems, tape the design onto your work surface. Lay the background fabric over the design, matching the centres, and tape the corners of the fabric. With a pencil, trace the outer line of the stems onto the background. (The outer line is indicated by the solid line; do not mark the dotted line. You only need one side marked as a guide for placing the stems.) If you cannot see the design clearly through your fabric, use a light-box or tape the design to a window.

4 Follow the instructions on page 18 to make the overlay and attach it to the background, matching the centre lines.

Bias bar stems – basic method

1 Set the sewing machine to a short stitch length, and thread it with a contrasting colour so that the stitching will show against the fabric.

2 Take a 1in bias strip and fold it in half, right sides out, along its length (**a**). With the folded edge of the strip to the right, machine a seam just over ⅛in from the fold. Use your machine foot as a guide, and stitch for a few inches, then check that the seam is the correct width.

Lift the presser foot and slide the bias bar into the channel you have made (**b**); it needs to be a snug fit. If it is too tight you will need to make a slightly wider seam; if it is too loose, make a slightly smaller seam. (Sometimes it's easier to make these fine adjustments by altering the needle position.) Lower the presser foot again and continue machining the strip. Remove the work from the machine.

3 Slide the bias bar into the seam; turn the seam so that it lays centrally down the middle of the bar (**c**), and press firmly. Remove the bar and press again from the back. If the strip is longer than the bar you will need to move the bar further along and repeat the procedure until the whole strip is pressed.

4 Replace the bar into the seam and trim the seam allowance close to the machine stitching. (This is why you need a short stitch length, to ensure that the seam doesn't collapse!) The contrasting thread helps you to see the machine stitching, which means that there is less likelihood of cutting the stitching by accident. I find it easier to do the trimming on the bar, but you can do it without the bar if you prefer. You obviously need to leave a very small seam allowance so that it doesn't extend beyond the width of the finished strip (**d**).

> **TIP** *I find it easier to press the seam and trim afterwards when making very narrow stems. However, for stems wider than ⅛in you can trim the seam allowance first and then press the strip on the bar.*

5 Pin the stem in position, placing the pins at right angles. You could use fabric glue (sparingly) on the back, to hold the stem in place; this is particularly helpful for very fine stems. Wider stems can be tacked down the centre. Work the needle-turn stitch down each side of the stem to secure it in place.

Appliqué

Stems

1 Make and appliqué the twining side stems using the bias bar method. Ensure that you leave enough extra at the end of each stem for the ends to be covered by the appliqué. You need to be particularly careful where there is a diagonal 'join' in the design between the stem and an appliqué shape; check with the overlay that you have left sufficient.

 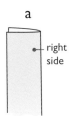

2 Make the foxglove stems, but do not appliqué these in place yet; add them only after leaf #15 and leaf #26 have been stitched in position (see below).

Leaves

1 Trace templates #1-#28 onto the freezer paper and cut them out, leaving pattern windows (see page 11).

2 Use the pattern windows to select the print area for each leaf; prepare and appliqué the leaves in number order. Remember that where an edge is covered by another leaf, that edge is not needle-turned under; leave it as a raw edge and simply secure it with a small running stitch (see page 29). One example of this is where leaf #20 is partially covered by leaf #21 and #22.

After you have stitched on leaf #15, appliqué the left-hand foxglove stem, and once you have stitched leaf #26, appliqué the right-hand foxglove stem.

3 Press the appliqué from the back before stitching on the flowers.

Flowers

Violets

1 These are made using the Suffolk Puff technique and a 1in circle of fabric (see page 36). As these are very small I suggest you work the running stitches before you cut out the circle; mark the circle on the fabric and use this as the guide for the stitching.

2 Make six violets, then divide each flower into five petals. Embroider a French knot in the centre of each flower.

3 Arrange the flowers on the background using the photograph as a guide. Pin them in place and sew them on from the back of the work (see page 41).

Primroses

1 The primroses are made using the ruched flower technique explained on page 40; in this instance, though, the strip is cut on the bias. The bias strip will have more 'give,' and will work better at this small size. Cut a ¾ x 3½in bias strip, and fold in the raw edges along the length to give a strip ⅜in wide; press.

2 Place the strip, with the raw edges uppermost, on the guide (**e**); mark it as indicated. Work small running stitches from dot to dot as

explained earlier (see page 40). Draw up the gathers to give you a 2in strip; fasten off the gathering thread and distribute the gathers evenly. Join as before to make the ruched flower.

3 To make the flower centres, use six strands of yellow embroidery floss and work four turkey stitches in the centre of the primrose. Work the loops over a turning stick (**f**) to keep the loops even in size (**g**). Cut the loops and fray out the cut threads (**h**); I used a rayon thread which I was able to tease out to make a fluffy centre.

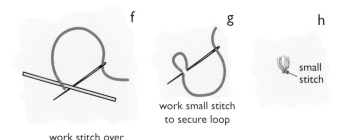

work stitch over turning stick — work small stitch to secure loop — small stitch

4 Make three primroses and appliqué them in position as shown (**i**). Make a smaller one using a 3in strip; this will make a four-petalled flower. Complete the flower as before and sew it in place (**j**).

Foxgloves

1 Cut templates A, B and C in plastic or card.

2 Use pencil to trace round the templates onto the wrong side of the foxglove outer fabric, leaving space for the seam allowances between the shapes. You will need four A shapes, six B shapes and four C shapes.

> ✎ **TIP** *The direction of the fabric grain is important here. Place one of the straight edges of each shape on the straight grain of the fabric, ie parallel with the selvedge; this will mean that the shape will be on the bias at the lower curved edge, which gives the flower a better shape.*

If you want to be particularly clever you can shade the flowers from darker to lighter as they get smaller. I used a batik with areas of different tones which I could use to advantage.

3 With right sides together, place the outer fabric on top of the lining fabric (**k**). Put a pin in the centre of each shape. Using a very small machine stitch, stitch *only* the lower curved seam of each flower

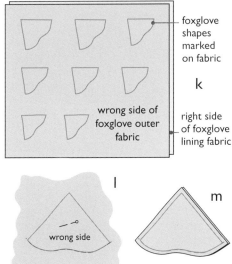

foxglove shapes marked on fabric

k

wrong side of foxglove outer fabric

right side of foxglove lining fabric

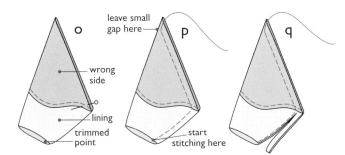

l

wrong side

m

(**l**). Extend the stitching for a stitch or two at each end beyond the seam line. Cut out the shapes adding ¼ in seam allowance (**m**).

4 Trim the curved seam close to the stitching; trim ⅝ in from the tip of the lining (**n**).

n

point trimmed away

5 Fold the flower in half, right sides together and matching seams; pin this point (**o**). Stitch the back seam of each flower, starting at the wide end and working towards the point (**p**). Stop just short of the point as shown to leave a small gap at top; leave the machine thread ends loose at the top, and trim the seam closely (**q**).

o

leave small gap here

p

q

wrong side

lining

trimmed point

start stitching here

6 Turn to the right side. I have tried various methods in the past to turn such small shapes and this has proved to be the easiest. Tie the threads at the top in a large needle and pass the needle, eye first, down inside the flower. Start to roll back the lining at

r

the wide end until you get to the point where you can pull the needle down and turn the rest of the flower through to the right side like magic (**r**)! To complete the flower, push the lining back inside the flower and finger-press the seam at the lower edge.

7 Make all the flowers in the same way. Starting at the base of each foxglove, arrange the flowers as shown. Note that the larger foxglove has two As, four Bs and two Cs (**s**). The smaller one has two As,

s   t

two Bs and two Cs (**t**). You may find it easier to work on a soft board or polystyrene tile while you are pinning the flowers in place.

8 Start stitching the As first and work your way up each foxglove. To attach each individual flower, put in a few strategic stitches initially, then use small stitches just under the side edges to keep them in place. As there are no raw edges there is nothing to hide!

u

9 Trace template D onto freezer paper; iron this shape onto the right side of the fabric and cut out. Appliqué two of these shapes at the top of each foxglove, overlapping them as shown in the photograph (**u**). Using two strands of green embroidery floss, work two or three lazy daisy stitches at the top of each foxglove (**v**).

10 Finally turn back the edge of some of the flowers to make a small cuff. They should stay in place, but if

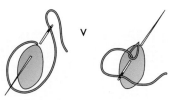

v

necessary anchor each one with a small stitch. As a final touch you could use a permanent marker pen to ink in some spots on the linings of the flowers.

❧ *Project 10* ❧

Nasturtium Wreath

I love the scrambling habit of nasturtiums as they spread through the flower beds in late summer; their brightly-coloured blooms were the inspiration for this dramatic wreath. To give them greater impact, I used a dark background for the appliqué. A dark background can present some problems but there are ways of overcoming them which I have explained in the instructions; it's worth the extra trouble, as a dark fabric can really make the appliqué glow. The little dimensional buds, as well as the embroidered and inked flower centres, add further interest to the design.

This is another block which works well on its own or could be combined with others in this book to make a larger quilt.

Techniques used

❧ working with dark backgrounds
❧ lining appliqué shapes
❧ dimensional buds
❧ inking details

FINISHED SIZE: the appliqué design measures approx 10in (25cm) square

The full-size templates and design for this project are on pages 94-95

What you will need

❧ 13in square background fabric (or larger if you prefer)

❧ appliqué fabrics:
   12in square orange/yellow for the flowers and buds
   12in square cream/yellow for lining the flowers
   9in square for the leaves and bud calyxes

The Appliqué Garden

- fine thread to match the appliqué fabrics
- yellow and dark red stranded embroidery floss
- Straw #11 needle for appliqué
- Crewel #6 needle for embroidery
- 11in square lightweight interfacing for the overlay
- freezer paper for templates
- brown or black Pigma™ 0.1 pen

Preparation

1 Fold the background fabric and tack the centre lines as described on page 11.

2 Trace the two sections of the full-size design onto paper, carefully matching the centre lines to create the complete design.

3 Follow the instructions on page 18 to make the overlay and attach it to the background, matching the centre lines.

Appliqué

Make freezer paper templates for all the numbered shapes and cut them out leaving pattern windows (see page 11). Don't forget to number the shapes and the windows! If you would like to make dimensional versions of the buds, as in my original and as described below, you won't need templates for the buds themselves.

Leaves

Use the pattern windows to select the print area for each leaf; I chose a batik fabric to suggest dappled sunshine falling on the leaves. Appliqué leaves #1-#3. Remember that where an edge is covered by another piece, that edge is not needle-turned under; simply secure the raw edge with a small running stitch (see page 29). Appliqué the remaining leaves after the buds and calyxes are in position

Dimensional buds

I designed these little pleated buds after careful observation of the real buds. If you prefer you could make them as flat appliqué; simply trace off templates #4, #6 and #8 onto freezer paper and appliqué the buds as usual. Remember to leave raw edges at the base of each bud – these will be covered by the calyx.

1 To make a dimensional bud, use Template A and cut it out in fabric at the exact size: do not add any seam allowance.

2 Pleat the curved edge below the broken line only (**a**) to produce the shape shown below; stitch the pleats in place at the lower edge.

3 Use the overlay to position the bud on the background; check carefully that the pleated edge will be covered by the calyx. (Bear in mind that the calyx has quite a deep V.) Pin the bud in place. Turn under the outer edge – not the pleated base – to make a bud that will be slightly bigger than the drawn flat bud. Catch the edges of the bud in position; I've allowed a generous turning on this edge, so that the stitching can be further under the folded edge to create a more dimensional effect (**b**).

4 Appliqué the calyx (**c**); check back to page 15 to remind yourself how to deal with inner points.

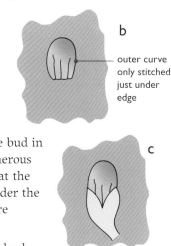

a

make small pleats on curved edge only up to broken line

b

outer curve only stitched just under edge

c

- **TIP** *I think that when you are working with a small shape such as this, the drawn line technique as shown in Basic Techniques is probably easier to manage than keeping the template in place and stitching around it. Feel free to use whichever method works best for you.*

Flowers

The flowers on this design introduce a new technique: lining the appliqué pieces. The flowers are lined for two reasons. First, when you are working on a dark fabric you tend to get 'show-through' of the seam allowances, and this can spoil the overall effect. Secondly, the lining produces a more dense colour as well as a slightly raised effect. I usually line all yellow flowers on any background anyway, as there always seems to be a tendency for the seam allowance to show through yellow fabric.

1 Use the pattern windows, not the templates, to cut out the lining for each flower. Start with #13. Iron the pattern window onto the right side of the lining fabric (**d**). With a pencil, draw round the inside of the window (**e**). Remove the window (**f**) and cut out the shape on the drawn line (**g**); this will make a shape slightly smaller than the original flower.

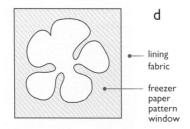

lining fabric

freezer paper pattern window

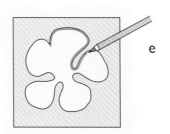

e

f

g

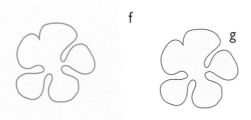

2 Use the overlay to position the lining on the background. Tack the shape in place (**h**) using a *light*-coloured thread; you do not want the stitching to show through – although it can be removed from the back later if necessary.

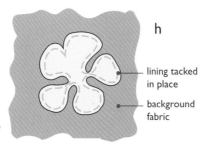

h

lining tacked in place

background fabric

3 When you are selecting the area of print for the nasturtiums, try to find shading that will indicate the overlapping of two of the petals. Again batiks work brilliantly here. You can see this more clearly in the close-up photo of the flower (**i**).

i

If you cannot achieve the same effect with your fabric, you could ink or embroider a dividing line as shown on the full-size design.

Position appliqué piece #13 using the overlay. Pin in the seam allowance (**j**) and tack the shape in place in the usual way; needle-turn the raw edges, turning the seam allowance under the lining (**k**). Appliqué all the flowers in the same way.

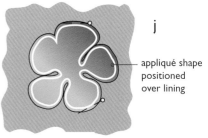

j

appliqué shape positioned over lining

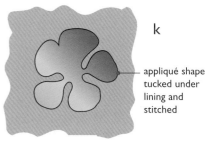

k

appliqué shape tucked under lining and stitched

Embellishing

l

Use the marking pen to ink in the petal markings as shown (**l**). Thicken up the base of the lines with stem stitch embroidered with one strand of dark red stranded embroidery floss (**m**).

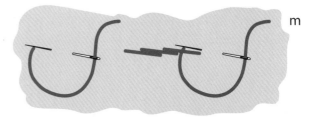

m

✑ Project 11 ✑

Daisy Chain

A daisy chain tied up with a blue ribbon bow gives a fresh country-style look to this block. Bordered with a check fabric it becomes a pretty cushion cover; it can also be combined with other blocks for larger projects. Although at first sight it looks quite a simple design, it does introduce several new techniques. The daisies are an example of my special method for making multi-petalled flowers without handling lots of small pieces. Padding the daisies also gives them more dimension.

The original shown in the photograph has an appliquéd bow; if you prefer, you could tie a ribbon bow and stitch it in place, leaving the ends free. Pretty little details like the scalloped edges on the dimensional buds add extra charm to the design.

Techniques used

- multi-petalled flowers
- padding appliqué shapes
- dimensional buds – another variation!
- bow (off-block construction)
- plastic overlays

FINISHED SIZE: the appliqué design measures approximately 10in (25 cm) square. The cushion measures 16in (approximately 41cm) square

The full-size templates and design for this project are on pages 96-98

What you will need

- 12in square background fabric (or larger if you prefer)
- appliqué fabrics:
    8in square of white for the flowers and buds
    small pieces of two tones of blue for the ribbon
    small piece of green for the bud calyxes
    small piece of yellow for the flower centres
    four 1 x 7in bias strips in dark green
    four 1 x 7in bias strips in medium green
- fine thread to match appliqué fabrics
- green stranded embroidery floss
- Straw #11 needle for appliqué
- Crewel #6 needle for embroidery
- 11in square lightweight interfacing for the overlay
- freezer paper for templates
- 8in square of very flat wadding
- ⅛in wide bias bar (or electrical tie – see page 51)
- To make the design into a cushion cover you will also need:
    four 1 x 12in strips of fabric for the inner border
    two 3 x 12in and two 3 x 17in strips of fabric for the outer border (see Borders, pages 72-74)
    18in square low-loft wadding
    18in square backing fabric
    18 x 22in fabric for the cushion back (see page 23 for how to make up the cushion cover)

Preparation

1 Fold the background fabric and tack the centre lines as described on page 11.

2 Trace the two sections of the full-size design onto paper, carefully matching the centre lines to create the complete design.

3 Follow the instructions on page 18 to make the overlay and attach it to the background, matching the centre lines. Remember to mark the registration dots on the daisies.

Appliqué

Stems

1 Make the stems using the bias bar method described on page 51.

2 Appliqué the stems in position; check with the overlay that you are placing them correctly – it can be a bit confusing with the twisting of the two stems. Note that the stems need normally only extend ⅛in under the daisies; be careful, though, as because of the angle of the stem and petal the stem may need to extend further to ensure that the raw end is covered (see the dotted line on the design). It's better to leave a generous amount to start with, and then trim back before finally stitching the daisy in position.

You will need to stitch both the dark and the medium stems simultaneously so that you can weave the stems over and under each other as shown on the design.

Bow

The bow is an example of off-block construction (also known as unit appliqué). This is a method used to pre-assemble some of the appliqué pieces before stitching them to the background. It's very useful in the construction of complex flowers and birds, and it's also useful when you are handling small shapes, as you can work on a larger piece of fabric and trim back the seam after stitching. This may seem a little confusing, but follow the step-by-step photos and it will become clearer.

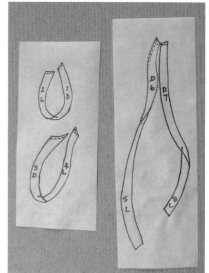

a

1 To make the templates, trace the whole bow onto freezer paper and cut the shapes apart – you do not need to make windows as there is no need to fussy-cut. Ensure that you mark the registration marks as shown on the loops and ties (**a**).

The eight pieces that make up the bow are quite narrow. You will probably find it easier to draw round the templates with a white marking pen (see page 12) and turn the fabric under to a drawn line, rather than keeping the template in place while needle-turning the bow to the background. The bow is made in two tones of fabric to create the effect of a right side and a reverse side to the ribbon, which makes it more realistic. Do not iron on the templates yet, but when you do come to that stage, check that you are using the correct tone for each template: #2, #4, #5 and #8 are made in the lighter tone; #1, #3, #6 and #7 are made in the darker tone.

2 To make the right-hand loop, iron template #1 onto dark fabric and cut it out in the usual way. Draw round the template and peel it back partially so that you can see the seam line (**b**). Place the shape onto a piece of lighter-tone fabric. Make a small clip on the inner curve – this will make it easier to needle-turn the small seam which joins #1 to #2 (**c**). Stitch this seam.

b

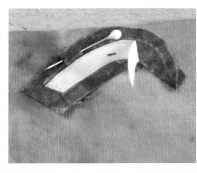

c

🕊 **TIP** *When you are stitching unit appliqué it's useful to make a plastic overlay so that you can check that you are positioning the appliqué pieces accurately. Use a fine black liner to trace the bow onto a piece of clear plastic.*

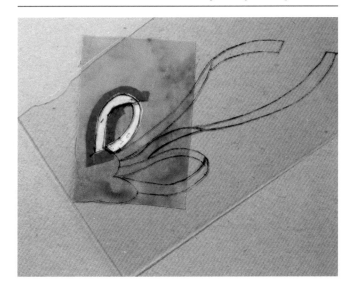

d

e

3 Iron template #2 in position (**d**). Draw round the template and cut out the shape, leaving the normal seam allowance (**e**). Turn the work over and trim back the seam closely (**f**). (You can trim quite closely as the seam has already been stitched. This is another advantage of off-block construction.) Finally, position the assembled loop onto the background using the main overlay as a positioning guide. Pin in the seam allowance and remove the templates. As this is such a narrow shape you can't really tack it in place; just leave a couple of pins in the opposite edge to where you are needle-turning (**g**). Once one side is attached the shape will not shift while you sew the second side.

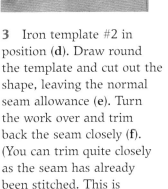

f

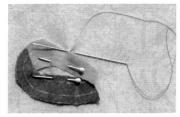

g

Note how you can smoothly turn both seam allowances under together as you stitch round the loop; this makes a very neat edge. Make the left-hand loop in a similar way.

4 Make the ties of the bow in a similar way. Stitch prepared #7 onto a light piece of fabric. Then position template #8 (**h**). In this way you will get the correct pieces looking as if they are coming forward, as though the ribbon is twisted.

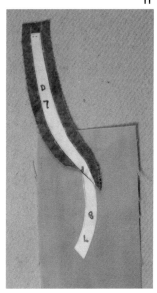

h

Daisies

The daisies introduce two new techniques: padded appliqué, and multi-petalled flower technique. As with the nasturtium flowers, lining the daisies will prevent 'show-through' of the seam allowances, which otherwise is likely to happen as the daisies are made from white fabric. You could simply line the daisies with a piece of white fabric, but using wadding creates a more dimensional effect and gives greater definition to the petals.

Padded appliqué

i

1 Trace off each **complete** daisy shape onto freezer paper (note the little registration dots), and cut out the shape to make a pattern window. Use the pattern windows, not the templates, to cut out the wadding for each flower. Place each window onto the wadding and very lightly iron it in place (**i**).

j

Lightly mark the little registration dots on the appropriate petals, then cut round the wadding inside the window; this will make a shape slightly smaller than the original daisy (**j**). If you do not have a non-stick sheet, you could just draw round inside the window; it's difficult, though, to draw an accurate, visible line on wadding. Making little dots with a Pigma™ pen works quite well.

2 Use the overlay to position the wadding shapes on the background. If you mark a registration dot on the overlay and on the wadding, this will help you to line up each shape easily. When shapes are not quite symmetrical you can waste a lot of time turning them round to find the correct position!

3 Tack the shapes in place using a light-coloured thread. You do not want the stitching to show through – although it can be removed from the back later if necessary.

Multi-petalled flowers – a neat trick

This is a useful technique when you are stitching a flower with many similar petals; I have used it for several types of flowers. The basic principle is to have some of the petals joined at the centre so that they can be stitched down as one unit. You get some rather strange-shaped templates, but it all works out in the end. For clarity, I have used a coloured fabric rather than white on the photographs, so that you can see exactly what is happening to the fabric, the wadding and the background.

Because several petals are cut at the same time with this technique, it's not really possible to 'fussy-cut' the shapes so that the light and shade is consistent on each petal – for this reason you don't need to cut pattern windows from the template. As the daisy fabric is white, of course, you don't need to worry about shading on the petals in this design!

k

1 Trace template #9 onto freezer paper – remember to add the registration dot. Cut the shape out in fabric adding the usual seam allowance. Use the overlay as a guide for positioning the shape over the wadding on the background. Needle-turn the outer edges of the petal as shown (**k**), turning the seam under the wadding on the outer edges of the flower. Where a dotted line is shown, do not needle-turn but leave this as a raw edge; it will be covered later by #10.

l

2 Using template #10, appliqué this shape on top of #9 (**l**). Again, turn the seam under the wadding on the outer edge of the shape. You will need to make a snip in the seam allowance at the base of the inner curve (see page 14); do not worry too much if this is a little untidy, as the daisy centre will cover it. When you are stitching #10, it helps to stitch at least through to the wadding where petals overlap. You will then get a more 'quilted' look and better definition of the petals.

Now you can see how with just two templates you have been able to make an eight-petalled flower. While this

is not exactly speed stitching, it does mean you have larger pieces to handle than eight little petals! Make the three other eight-petalled daisies in the same way.

3 The remaining side-view daisies have nine petals, but they can still be assembled using the above technique. You simply need to stitch down one single petal first before adding the 'joined up' petals. I've used the flower created from templates #21-23 to demonstrate the principle.

Work over the wadding shape tacked to the background (**m**). Appliqué petal #21 (**n**), needle-turning the outer edge only and leaving the edges raw where they will be covered by another shape. Appliqué #22

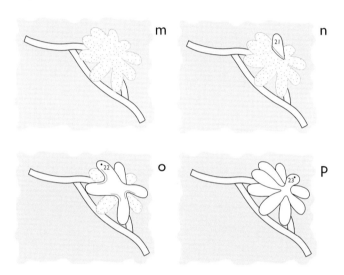

in the same way as before – only needle-turning the outer edges and tucking the seam allowance under the wadding (**o**). Appliqué #23 on top in a similar way as for the eight-petalled daisy (**p**). You do not have to too fussy about the inner curve at the base of the petals as it will be covered by the centre (**q**).

Daisy centres

1 The round daisy centres can be made using the perfect circle method (see page 17) and a ½in circle template.

2 You can make the oval daisy centre in a similar way but you will need to cut a card template. Trace daisy centre #24 from the design onto freezer paper – do not cut it out at this stage. Iron the piece of freezer paper onto card, then cut out the shape on the drawn line; this will produce a more accurate template. Cut the fabric ¼in bigger and work a small gathering stitch around the raw edge. Pull up the fabric over the card

in the same way as when making a perfect circle. Press very firmly; remove the card and appliqué in the usual way to the centre of the daisy.

Dimensional buds

1 Cut a 1½ x 1in piece of white fabric; fold it in half, right side out (**a**). Using white thread, scallop the folded edge as described below. (Once again, I've used a coloured thread on the diagrams so that you can see how the technique works.)

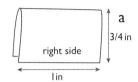

Start ¼in from the edge, and insert the needle just below the fold. Wrap the thread over the edge and bring the needle up in the same place

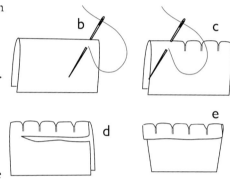

(**b**); pull the thread tightly and work a small stitch on the back to lock the stitch. Move the needle along ⅛in and work the next overcast stitch; make four scallops in the same way (**c**). Trim the seam closely on the back (**d**), and also trim the sides slightly (**e**).

2 Trace the calyx template onto freezer paper; cut out the shape and iron it onto the calyx fabric. Cut out the fabric adding ⅛in seam allowance. Turn under ⅛in along the top straight edge (**f**), and scallop the edge to make four scallops ⅛in apart (**g**).

3 Appliqué the top of the calyx shell to the white section, placing the calyx ½in below the top of the corresponding section of white fabric (**h**). Trim away the surplus white fabric on the back.

4 Appliqué the assembled bud to the background, changing the thread colour as necessary (**i**).

Embroidery

Embroider the bud stems using stem stitch (see page 56) and two strands of dark green stranded embroidery floss.

Summer Bounty

One of the treats of an English summer is a strawberry or raspberry picked straight from the garden. While I can't capture the gorgeous flavour in appliqué, I think that these plump raspberries look good enough to eat! A field hedge runs alongside my garden and in summer it is smothered with the delicate pink flowers of the briar roses. The roses happily scramble through the hedge and never seem to get attacked by the dreaded greenfly!

These appliquéd roses have pretty dimensional centres and introduce a new technique for handling really tiny pieces to get sharp points on the sepals. A few small dimensional Suffolk Puff flowers and embroidered details add the finishing touches to this charming block that is so evocative of summer.

Techniques used

~ dimensional raspberries

~ dimensional flower centres

~ sharp points on small pieces

FINISHED SIZE: the appliqué design measures approx 10½in (approx 26cm) square

The full-size templates and design for this project are on pages 99-101

What you will need

~ 13in square background fabric (or larger if you prefer)

~ appliqué fabrics:
 shaded pink for the rose flowers
 small pieces of yellow and green for the rose centres
 three or more greens for the leaves
 small piece of brown for the stem
 very pale pink/cream for the small flowers
 raspberry-red for the raspberries
 red and a small piece of green for the strawberries

~ fine threads to match the appliqué fabrics

~ regular sewing threads to match the raspberries, rose centre and small flowers

~ medium green, olive green, dark green and yellow stranded embroidery floss

~ Straw #11 needle for appliqué

~ Crewel #6 needle for embroidery

~ 11in square lightweight interfacing for the overlay

~ freezer paper for templates

~ small piece of very thin wadding

~ small amount of polyester stuffing

~ brown Pigma™ pen 0.1

Preparation

1 Fold the background fabric and tack the centre lines as described on page 11.

2 Trace the two sections of the full-size design onto paper, carefully matching the centre lines to create the complete design.

3 Follow the instructions on page 18 to make the overlay and attach it to the background, matching the centre lines.

Appliqué

1 Appliqué the brown stem sections and all the leaves in number order (#1-#33). Remember not to needle-turn the edges which are covered by another shape; leave these edges raw. As the stem sections are so small, I recommend using the drawn line method (see page 12) rather than keeping the paper template in place while needle-turning.

Rose

1 Appliqué petals #34 and #35. The remaining petals (template #36) are appliquéd as one piece. Use the pattern window and try to select an area of shading which will suggest the 'break' in the petals (**a**). Appliqué the two other full-view roses in position in the same way.

a

2 For the flower centre, cut a 4 x ⅜in strip of yellow fabric on the straight grain. Work running stitch along one long edge, then fray out the opposite long edge to a depth of ¼in (**b**). Pull up the running stitch to gather the strip into a circle (**c**), and stitch it in the middle of the rose.

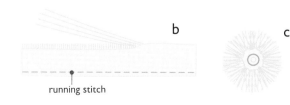

b c

running stitch

Using template A, cut the rose centre out of green fabric. Turn a very small hem to the wrong side around the edge of the circle (**d**), securing it with a small running stitch. Pull the shape up tightly and fasten off the thread (**e**); stitch the shape in the centre of the frayed circle.

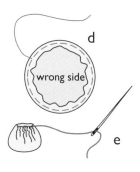

This technique for working dimensional centres can be used for many different flowers.

Side-view rose

I've devised this method to make it easier to handle the very small sepals. It also enables you to achieve very sharp points: be prepared to amaze your fellow quilters! The method involves positioning folded pieces of the sepal fabric on the petals; using the folded edge means that there is only the outer raw edge to deal with. Use reasonably large pieces which will be easier to handle; you will cut the surplus away afterwards.

You may find that it helps to make a plastic overlay just for the side-view roses. This is particularly helpful if you prefer to use the off-block construction method to assemble the complete side-view rose (see the instructions for making the bow for *Daisy Chain* on page 58). Trace these roses onto the plastic using an overhead marker or other fine black liner (**a**). Use this overlay to check that you have the small pieces correctly positioned as you assemble the rose; it will be more accurate than using the main overlay, and you will be able to see what you are doing more clearly.

───────────────

✎ **TIP** *It also helps to put registration marks on the templates and pattern windows where shapes meet (**d**).*

───────────────

1   Start with petal #43. Make the freezer paper template by tracing #43 and #44 together as one template (**b**).

Place the pattern window on the right side of the rose fabric and select the area of print to use. Slide a piece of folded green fabric under the window with the folded edge showing through. Matching the registration marks (see tip), position the green fabric to create a sepal #44 (**c** and **d**).

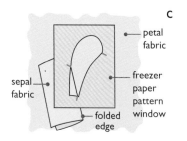

Remove the window and pin the green fabric to the pink fabric.

Stitch the folded edge in place (**e** and **f**) – check the correct positions to start and finish the stitching with the aid of the window.

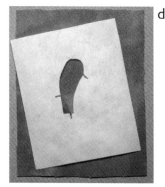

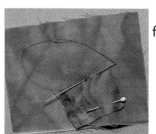

folded edge stitched

2   Trim the freezer paper template to leave #43 (**g**). Place the window back in position and place template #43 in the window, lining it up correctly with #44 which is already stitched in place (**h** and **i**).

sepal trimmed away

registration marks

petal template replaced in pattern window

Iron the template in place and cut out the shape adding the seam allowance (**j** and **k**); trim the seam closely (**l**).

freezer paper template

Make petal #46 in the same way (**m**).

46

45

3 To make petal #49 you will need to make two inserts of folded green fabric. 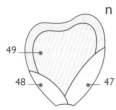  Proceed as before, but position the green strip for #47 first, then #48. Note that the two inserts overlap at the base (**n** and **o**).

4 Photo **p** shows the three petals prepared ready for appliqué.  Appliqué the petals in position, either keeping the templates in place or using the drawn line method (see page 12). You will need to change thread colour as you stitch so that you are using the appropriate colour each time. If you are using a plastic overlay, use it to check the shape of the flower as you stitch. 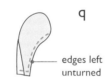 Swing under the green and pink seam allowances together to get a smooth edge; remember not to needle-turn the edge which will be covered by another petal (**q**).

edges left unturned

5 Once all the petals are stitched in place (**r**),  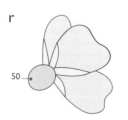 appliqué #50 (**s**). This will neatly cover the raw edges at the base of the flower and sepals. Make the second side-view rose in the same way.

50

6 An alternative approach to this technique is shown in photo **t**. 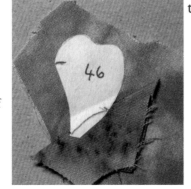 Iron the petal template onto a piece of pink fabric. Peel back the edge and insert underneath a folded piece of green fabric, lining it up with the registration marks. Appliqué the folded green edge to the pink fabric, then iron the template back in place; cut out the shape and proceed as before.

You have now completed the more challenging parts of *Summer Bounty*, and mastered a new technique which you will find useful in the future. This technique could be very helpful in miniature work.

Strawberries

The strawberries are appliquéd in the usual way. I was able to find a mottled red fabric which had just the right texture for the strawberries when I used a pattern window to pick the best sections. If you are not so lucky you could work little stitches with a fine yellow thread to suggest the seeded surface. You will notice that I've even included a little pale green unripe berry.

Raspberries

These are really fun to make and will always intrigue admirers of your work!

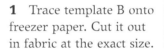

1 Trace template B onto freezer paper. Cut it out in fabric at the exact size.

2 On the wrong side of the fabric shape, draw circles as shown on the template.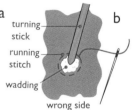

turning stick
running stitch
wadding
wrong side

Using matching regular sewing thread, fasten on securely and work small running stitches around circle #1 (**a**). Place a snippet (about ¼in square) of thin wadding on the circle; hold it in place with the tip of a turning stick (**b** and **c**) and pull up the stitches tightly, removing the stick once you've pulled the circle taut. Work a back stitch, then move over to circle #2. Work a little back stitch to get started, and then running stitch around the circle;  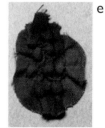 stuff and pull up as before. Proceed in this way until all the circles are stitched (**d** shows the reverse side and **e** the right side).

3 Work a small running stitch around the entire outer edge of the shape (**f**). Pull the thread up slightly to produce a raspberry shape about 1in long; insert a little stuffing to make a plump berry (**g** and **h**). Appliqué the raspberry in position as shown in the design. If you don't feel confident doing this by eye, you could trace the raspberry shape from the full-size design and

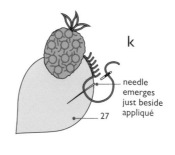

make a template. Draw round the template to mark the raspberry position on the background using a pencil or white marking pen. Try to 'nip' in the edge as you sew so that you get an irregular edge rather than a smooth one.

4 Make three more raspberries in the same way. Make a smaller one by using template C and working fewer circles. A smaller one fits better into the space – four large ones might look rather heavy.

Small raspberry flowers

These are made using the Suffolk Puff flower technique (page 36). Cut a circle of fabric using template A (the same one that you used for the rose centre). Gather the circle and divide it into five petals, then embroider a French knot in the centre using two strands of yellow embroidery floss (**i**).

Embellishing

Embroidery

1 Embroider the leaf stems using stem stitch and two strands of medium green embroidery floss.

2 Embroider the strawberry stems in a similar way. Work three lazy daisy stitches at the top of each strawberry (**j**), using three strands of embroidery floss; work a straight stitch in the centre of each loop to fill the stitch.

3 Use olive green stranded embroidery floss to embroider sepals at the top of each raspberry.

4 Use one strand of embroidery floss and work blanket stitch around the raspberry leaves. Slant the stitches as shown in the diagram (**k**) and the photograph (**l**).

Inking
Use brown Pigma™ pen to ink in the brown thorns on the rose stem.

Quilting
When the block is prepared for quilting, quilt the central vein lines on the raspberry and strawberry leaves; also quilt the petal division lines on #36, #39 and #42.

✧ *Variation* ✧

You can create other dimensional fruits using a similar technique to that used for the raspberries. My *Bullfinch and Blackberries* design (see Resources on page 79) features dimensional blackberries made using a 1¼in circle of fabric. Gather it up in the same way as for the dimensional raspberries, using template D on page 99 for guidance.

Project 13
Woodpecker

The green woodpecker is one of the more colourful British birds and is a frequent visitor to my garden. He can often be seen digging for food on the lawn, or heard drilling holes in the nearby telegraph pole! In this quilt the woodpecker is encircled by a wreath of leaves as his long beak makes a hole in a tree-trunk. This is an example of a framed design, with a scene within the frame; the background of quilted leaves echoes the woodland theme. The pattern windows are very helpful in the search for just the right shading for the woodpecker; check in a bird book for the correct colouring if you are not lucky enough to have a woodpecker in your garden.

The hole which the woodpecker is busy making is stitched using reverse appliqué. Don't be put off by the idea of reverse appliqué: the stitching method is very similar to the usual needle-turning technique, but in this case you are working with the appliqué fabric underneath, showing through an aperture cut in the top fabric layer. This top layer is usually the background fabric, but in this particular design the top layer is the tree-trunk fabric.

Techniques used

∾ reverse appliqué

∾ fused appliqué

FINISHED SIZE: the appliqué design measures approximately 10½in (approximately 21cm) square. The finished quilt measures 19¼in (39cm) square.

The full-size templates and design for this project are on pages 102-104

What you will need

∾ 14in square background fabric

∾ 9in square for the inner background behind the woodpecker

∾ appliqué fabrics:
  three or more greens for the leaves
  brown for the tree-trunk
  greens and red for the woodpecker (use the photograph as a guide for the colours required)

∾ ¼ yd (0.25m) fabric for the inner border

∾ ⅛ yd (0.5m) fabric for the outer border and binding

∾ brown Ultrasuede[R] for the beak (or this can be embroidered)

∾ fabric glue

∾ small black bead for the eye

∾ fine threads to match the appliqué fabrics

∾ red, black and brown stranded embroidery floss

∾ Straw #11 needle for appliqué

∾ Crewel #6 needle for embroidery

∾ 12in lightweight interfacing for the overlay

∾ freezer paper for templates

∾ black Pigma™ pen 0.1

∾ to complete the quilt:
  20in square low-loft wadding
  20in square backing fabric

Preparation

1 Fold the background fabric and tack the centre lines as described on page 11.

2 Trace the two sections of the full-size design onto paper, carefully matching the centre lines to create the complete design.

3 Follow the instructions on page 18 to make the overlay and attach it to the background, matching the centre lines.

Appliqué

∾ **TIP** *I've used a slightly different background fabric for the inner circle which is appliquéd behind the woodpecker. If you prefer, you could omit this piece and simply appliqué the tree-trunk and bird straight onto the main background fabric.*

The Appliqué Garden

Tree-trunk

1 Trace onto freezer paper the separate template given for the tree-trunk (#1). Note that the shape of this piece follows the outer edge of the circle and not the shape of the leaves. Trace the hole (template #2) on template #1 in the position indicated.

2 Cut out the template, leaving a pattern window as usual so that you can select the most effective area of print on the fabric. Iron the template in position and cut out in the normal way. Cut out the hole (#2) as well, but remember to add on the usual seam allowance (**a**).

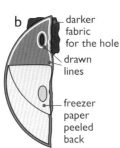

3 Pin a small piece of darker fabric under the hole and reverse appliqué the shape. You can either keep the freezer paper template in place or use a drawn line (see page 12); I like to use a drawn line for reverse appliqué. You could just partly peel back the template to do the reverse appliqué and leave part in place for the next stage (**b**). You will need to make snips in the seam allowance to achieve an accurate shape. Remember to snip only half the depth of the seam allowance first of all; you can always cut a little deeper if you find that the edge will not turn under smoothly.

(labels b): darker fabric for the hole; drawn lines; freezer paper peeled back

Work running stitch ½in outside the marked line; this helps to stabilise the work as you turn under the seam allowance around the hole (**c**). Needle-turn the edge in the usual way; once the appliqué is complete, trim back the dark fabric close to the stitching on the reverse side (**d**).

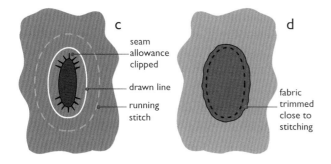

(labels c): seam allowance clipped; drawn line; running stitch
(labels d): fabric trimmed close to stitching

4 Trace the circle from the design onto freezer paper; cut out the shape and use it as a template to cut out in fabric for the inner background circle. (Omit the instructions relating to this shape if you are not using a different fabric for the centre circle.)

5 Position the tree-trunk on the fabric circle, using the overlay for guidance, and tack it in place (**e**).

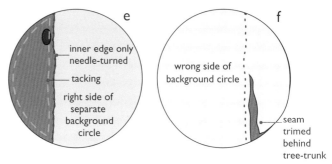

(labels e): inner edge only needle-turned; tacking; right side of separate background circle
(labels f): wrong side of background circle; seam trimed behind tree-trunk

Appliqué only along the straighter edge of the trunk. Cut away the circle fabric behind the trunk, leaving a ¼in seam allowance (**f**).

Woodpecker

1 Make templates in freezer paper and use the pattern window technique to aid your fabric selection; use the main photograph as a guide for the colour shading. Appliqué the woodpecker shapes in number order. You will need to line up the circle under the overlay to position the woodpecker pieces – or if you prefer you could make a separate plastic overlay for the bird (see the technique used for the rose in *Summer Bounty* on page 64). In this case, assemble the woodpecker as unit appliqué, then use the main overlay to position it on the circle.

2 The red head markings (#5) may be needle-turned, but as this is a small shape you may find it easier to bond the shape in place using fusible web, and then work blanket stitch with one strand of red embroidery thread around the raw edge. This is how I created the original. I also added a few additional straight stitches at the back of the head (**g**), which helps to neaten the edge at this point.

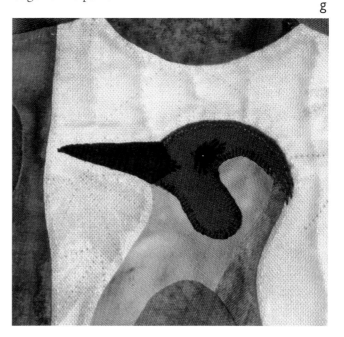

3 Cut the beak in Ultrasuede[R] (or other non-fray fabric), and glue it in position. Secure with tiny stitches. Alternatively you could embroider the beak.

4 Embroider the legs using rows of stem stitch worked with two strands of brown embroidery floss.

5 Sew on a bead for the eye and add a few straight stitches in black as shown on photograph **g** on page 69. Press the work on the reverse side.

Inner circle

1 Use the overlay to position the circle on the background square.

2 Attach the shape with small running stitches around the outer edge of the circle (**h**).

h

right side of
background fabric

Leaves

1 Appliqué leaves #8-#11 first, then the remaining leaves in number order. The leaves need to just cover the raw edge of the inner circle. Be careful where two leaves butt up together, eg #14 and #17.

2 Use two strands of brown embroidery floss to embroider the corner leaf stems in stem stitch.

3 Lay the completed appliqué right side down on a well-padded surface, and press on the reverse side.

Finishing

Borders

1 Trim the background to 13½in square.

2 Cut the borders as follows:

two 1½ x 13½in strips for the sides of the inner border

two 1½ x 15½in strips for the top and bottom of the inner border

two 2½ x 15½in strips for the sides of the outer border

two 2½ x 19½in strips for the top and bottom of the outer border

3 Using ¼in seams throughout, add the side pieces of the inner border; press the seams away from the central block. Add the top and bottom borders, again pressing the seams away from the block.

4 Attach the outer borders in the same way.

Quilting

1 Prepare the quilt sandwich (see page 74) using the appliquéd design, the wadding and the backing fabric.

Tips for fused appliqué
(using fusible web)

1 Back a small piece of red fabric with fusible web, ironing the adhesive side to the wrong side of the fabric.

2 Make a freezer paper template using the separate template #5 given on page 104. Iron the template onto the right side of the fabric.

3 Cut out the shape to the exact size, without adding a seam allowance. Remove the paper backing, then use the overlay to position the piece on the woodpecker shape.

4 Iron the shape to stick it in place. (Fusible web can mess up the iron and your ironing surface, if the iron comes in contact with the adhesive. If you use fusible web a lot, it's a good idea to cover the area with a non-stick baking sheet or an appliqué pressing sheet to avoid this problem.)

TIP *Before preparing the design for quilting, you may like to cut away the background fabric behind the inner circle. It is easier to hand quilt through only one layer of top fabric. Take care though – you do not want to cut through the top layer of fabric as well!*

2 Closely outline the appliqué design with hand quilting (see page 74). Quilt irregular lines on the inner circle to suggest distant trees.

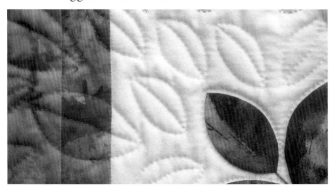

3 Use the leaf templates, in varying sizes, as guides for quilting leaf shapes randomly over the quilt. You could tack or pin the leaf templates in place as a guide for quilting, iron them lightly in place, or use a hera (see page 9) to mark round the templates.

Binding

Trim the quilt to an accurate rectangle, and follow the instructions on page 75 to bind the edges.

The
Finishing Touches

Having put so much time and effort into stitching your appliqué design, it deserves extra care to make it into a stunning quilt. This section takes you through the finishing stages, and gives you lots of tips for constructing a quilt to be proud of!

Pressing

Press the work from the back on a well-padded surface. The background areas around the appliqué may be pressed more heavily, even on the right side, but press the appliqué only lightly. Heavy pressing or over-pressing will flatten the texture and cause the seam allowances to leave an impression on the surface of the appliqué; this rather spoils the finished effect that you have created so carefully. Cover the work with a Teflon™ pressing cloth to protect the appliqué.

Sizing

1 A 15in square ruler is very useful for squaring up the work accurately. You can trim the block accurately using a rotary cutter on a cutting mat. Ensure that the square ruler is placed centrally on the block. (If you are following a specific pattern, don't forget to check whether seam allowance is included in the trimmed size.)

2 If the block has lots of dimensional details this can make it difficult to lay the square ruler flat on the surface of the appliqué. To avoid this problem, cut a card template the required block size (including seam allowance). Mark a 1in border, and cut out the inner square to leave a central hole. Mark the centre on each side of the card. You now have a window that you can place centrally over the block (**a**).

Draw round the outer edge of the card template. Remove the card template and trim the block on the drawn line. This is another great tip from Nancy Kerns.

3 If you have more than one block in the quilt, join the blocks with ¼in seams.

Setting the blocks

Single blocks or combinations of blocks may be set and bordered in different ways. I've given you some ideas with these examples; try experimenting with different layouts.

Borders and sashings

It's always worth 'auditioning' various fabrics for borders and sashings. Fold the fabrics so that the appropriate amount of each fabric shows against the quilt. If you have a design wall it's useful to pin the fabrics up and stand back to consider the colour combinations (**b**).

a

b

The appliqué is the more important part of the quilt, so you want the borders to frame the design and draw the eye in to the appliqué. I often use a narrow inner border using one of the appliqué fabrics, and then a wider outer border which reflects the general colour-scheme but is not too dominant (eg as for *Blue Vase* on page 39).

When you are adding borders or sashings, press all seams away from the blocks so that the turnings don't show through the background fabric on the right side.

Sashings

You may like to have sashing strips between the blocks as in the *Apples* quilt (see page 26). The exact width of the sashing will depend on the size of the blocks, but a finished width of 1-1¼in would suit most designs. Add the sashings in the order shown (**a**).

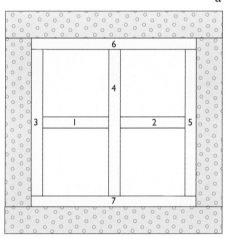

Narrow borders

1 A ¼in narrow inner border really sets off the appliqué – a bit like a double mount for a photograph or picture. The disadvantage is that with such a narrow border, it's only too easy to see any unevenness in the width. The method I use overcomes this problem.

2 Cut a strip of fabric 1in wide and the required length. Press the strip accurately in half, right side out.

3 Open out the strip and pin it to a side edge of your quilt or block, right sides together and matching the raw edges (**a**). Machine along the fold line (**b** and **c**); this will give you a ½in seam.

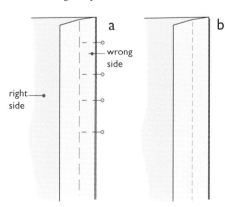

4 Fold the strip in half over the machine stitching (**d** and **e**). Repeat steps 2 and 3 to attach a narrow border to the opposite side of the quilt. Finally cut two strips the required length for the top and bottom edges and attach them in the same way (**f**).

5 Place one of the outer border side strips on top of the narrow border, right sides together. Turn the work to the wrong side. Pin the outer border in place, keeping the outer edges together (**g**).

6 Machine ¼in from the first row of stitching (**h** and **i**).

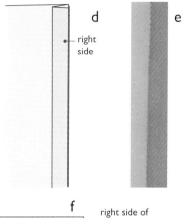

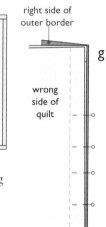

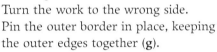

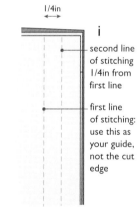

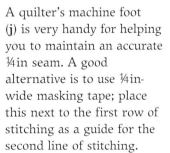

A quilter's machine foot (**j**) is very handy for helping you to maintain an accurate ¼in seam. A good alternative is to use ¼in-wide masking tape; place this next to the first row of stitching as a guide for the second line of stitching.

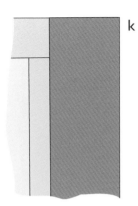
k

l

7 From the right side, press the seam turnings towards the border. You now have an accurate inner border sandwiched between the block and the outer border (**k** and **l**).

8 Add the outer border to the opposite side in the same way, and then add the top and bottom borders (**m**).

m

Depending on the way you are going to quilt the project, you may want to trace on a quilting design at this stage. I mark most of my quilting designs after the quilt has been layered as I mainly use a hera or templates; see my ideas for background quilting on the opposite page.

Wadding

A quilt has three layers: the top, the wadding and the backing. There are many brands and types of wadding, but for an appliquéd quilt, a flat, low-loft wadding works best. Hobbs Heirloom® cotton batting is a good example; Quilters Dream™ cotton (Request Loft) also works well. Some waddings need to be washed before you use them because they shrink – this is something to bear in mind if you intend to wash the finished quilt and do not want the crinkled, antique look that some people prefer.

1 Cut the wadding an inch bigger all round than the quilt top.

2 Cut the backing fabric the same size as the wadding.

❧ **TIP** *For ease of hand quilting, use a soft cotton fabric for the backing. Batiks, being tightly woven, are more difficult to hand quilt.*

---

3 Make the quilt 'sandwich.' Lay the backing fabric, right side down, on the work surface. Position the wadding on top, aligning the raw edges, and finally lay the on quilt top, right side up. Smooth out the layers, then pin the quilt sandwich in the centre and at the centre of each outer edge (**a**).

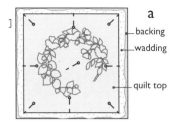
a
— backing
— wadding
— quilt top

4 If you intend to hand quilt the top, you will need to tack the layers together in a grid formation. If you intend to machine quilt, then use safety pins to hold the layers together. Start the tacking at the centre leaving a long tail of thread (**b**) – you can then re-thread the tail to tack in the opposite direction later. This method avoids having to keep fastening the tacking threads on and off. Tack the centre lines to start with, then complete the grid working outwards from the centre lines as shown in **c**.

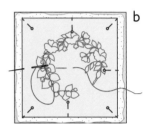
b

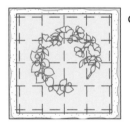
c

Quilting

1 I use regular cotton machine thread for hand quilting rather than the 'proper' quilting thread, as I find the latter rather thick. Experiment with different threads to see which you prefer. The *Oak and Acorn* cushion (see page 20) was hand quilted with a subtly variegated machine quilting thread.

2 Outline-quilt the appliqué design, stitching a scant ⅛in from the appliqué. This helps to bring the appliqué forward and gives it more dimension. You may need to quilt in any vein lines on leaves, division lines between petals, and possibly additional designs on large pieces such as vases; this gives large appliqué pieces more definition, and also helps to keep them flat (**a**).

a

The Appliqué Garden

3 There are various ways in which you can quilt the background of your design. The amount of quilting you use is your personal preference; however, the appliqué sits better if the background is fairly heavily quilted. Try to keep an even density of quilting over the whole quilt, including the borders, otherwise the quilt edges tend to flute and the quilt does not hang very well.

Background quilting ideas

1 A traditional pattern of square diamonds or diagonal lines is classic (**b**). Lines of this kind can be marked with the aid of a hera (**c**) so that there are no problems with removing pencil marks. If you have suitable spaces on the background, you could include feathers and other traditional motifs; just be careful that the quilting complements the appliqué and does not make it too busy.

2 Echo quilting also works well with appliqué. Work rows of quilting, echoing the outline of the appliqué design (see *Apples* on page 25 and *Blue Vase* on page 39). You can pin some of the templates that were used for the appliqué onto the background, or iron them in position very lightly, and incorporate these shapes into the echo quilting (**d**); I used this technique to quilt *Woodpecker* (**e**) and *Blue Vase* (**f**).

3 Try stitching French knots in a random pattern to create a stippled effect.

I just use a regular sewing thread, but you could use two strands of embroidery floss (**g**).

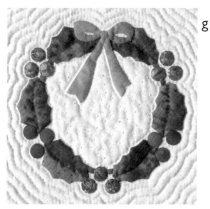

4 The background print may suggest a quilting pattern; you could quilt around the print for an attractive random effect (**h**).

5 Use the appliqué templates to create a quilting design. I used three oak leaves for the centre of *Autumn Glory* (see page 49). Pin or very lightly iron the templates in place and then quilt round their outlines. I used a similar idea to quilt the corners of the *Oak and Acorn* cushion (see page 23).

6 If you choose them well, you can use several different quilt patterns on one block. The *Geranium* block shown on the inside back cover has three different quilting patterns to suggest a context for the appliqué: pebbles on the ground, a low brick wall, and echo quilting for the distance.

7 If you prefer to machine quilt, then stipple quilting patterns work well with appliqué (see *Autumn Glory* on page 46).

Continuous binding

One of the challenges when binding a quilt is to achieve accurate mitred corners. This method, using a continuous binding strip, works well and creates very good mitres.

Preparation

1 Quilting tends to 'shrink' the work, and also to make the edges a little uneven, so once the quilting is complete, trim the quilt to an accurate rectangle.

2 Work running stitch around the edge to keep the layers together - you can also ease in any fullness at this stage if the quilt does not lie quite flat.

3 Now you need to work out the width of your binding strip. You can cut the binding single or double; I've given instructions for both.

Single binding

1 For a single binding, cut the strip of fabric four times the finished width plus an extra ⅛in; the extra allows for the take-up of fabric as the binding is folded over the thickness of the quilt. So, for a ¼in finished binding, the strip will need to be cut 1⅛in wide.

2 Cut the binding strips on the straight grain of the fabric (you only need to cut the strips on the bias if the edge of the quilt is curved and shaped). To determine the required length, measure round the quilt, then add on about 10in for the corner turns and joins. You will probably have to make at least one join to create a long enough strip.

3 Join the strips on the bias to give a flatter finish. Place two strips right sides together as shown (**a**), and use a short machine stitch to stitch a seam (**b**). (You may like to pencil in a line to keep your seam-line accurate.) Press the seam open and trim (**c**).

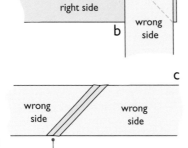

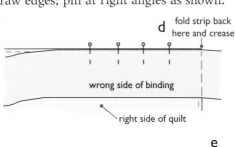

4 Begin in the centre of one side of the quilt. (Before you begin, it's a good idea to check where the joins in the strip will come on the quilt. Try to avoid having a join at a corner.) Lay the strip, right side down, on the front of the quilt along the edge, matching the raw edges; pin at right angles as shown. At the corner, fold back the binding level with the edge of the quilt and crease firmly (**d**).

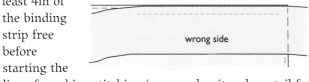

5 Leave at least 4in of the binding strip free before starting the line of machine stitching (you need quite a long tail for making the final join at the end). Taking a ¼in seam, machine the strip in place, stopping ¼in from the fold.

(The quilter's machine foot is very useful here as it has ¼in markings.) Secure with a few reverse stitches (**e**).

6 Fold up the strip diagonally so that the folded crease line lies along the edge (**f**). Now fold the strip down so that it lies along the adjacent edge (**g**). You will see that a diagonal fold has been formed under the strip, which will create a mitre at the corner. Pin the binding strip in place down the adjacent side, making a crease as before at the next corner. Re-start the machining from the top and finish ¼in from the crease as before.

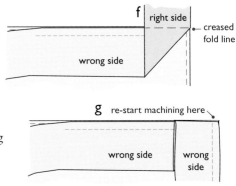

7 Continue in this way until you have turned all four corners. Machine part way on the final side, leaving a gap of at least 8in from where you started. You now need to join the ends of the strip before going any further. It's worth taking a little trouble with this join; it's only a little thing, but it can affect the hang of a small quilt.

8 Fold one end up at right angles; finger-press the fold. Fold up other end in the same way so that the strip is a snug fit (**h**). Place the two ends as shown (**i**), and machine on the creased line. Check the fit of the binding; you may have to re-stitch to get an exact fit. When you are sure it's correct, trim the seam and press it open. Pin the last part of the binding in place and machine the seam as before.

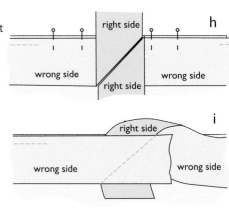

9 Finally fold the binding to the back, turning under ¼in and hemming the folded edge to the machine stitching. Arrange the folds in a mitre at each corner on the back (**j**).

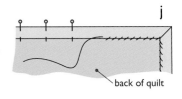

Double binding

1 If you prefer to make a double binding, the strip needs to be cut six times the finished width plus ¼in to allow for the thickness of the quilt. So for a ¼in finished binding, the strip will be cut 1¾in wide. Follow the guidelines given for a single binding to calculate the length of your binding, and to join strips on the bias to reach the required length.

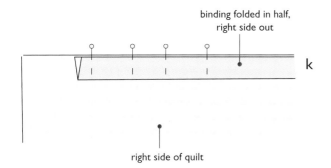

binding folded in half,
right side out

k

right side of quilt

2 Fold the binding strip in half, **wrong** sides together and raw edges matching (**k**). Machine the binding in place in the same way as for a single binding until you come to make the final join. At this stage, open out the binding to make the final seam on the bias; if you stitch through the folded strip it will create rather a lumpy seam. Turn the strip to the back of the quilt and hem the folded edge to the machine stitching – this stage is easier with a double binding than with a single binding.

Whichever method you have used, you should have a neat mitre at each corner of your quilt (**l**).

l

Hanging sleeves

A hanging sleeve is used so that you can display your wall quilt. If you enter your quilt for a show it will usually need a 4in sleeve; on small quilts I use a smaller sleeve appropriate to the size of the quilt.

1 Cut the sleeve twice the finished width plus an extra ½in for the seam; the length should be slightly less than the width of the quilt.

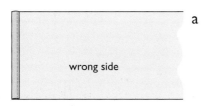

wrong side

a

Make a narrow hem at each end of the sleeve (**a**).

2 Fold the fabric in half with the **right** side outside and stitch a ¼in seam (**b**).

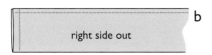

right side out

b

3 Press the sleeve so that the seam runs centrally down the back of the sleeve (**c**).

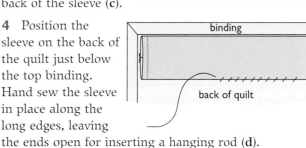

c

binding

back of quilt

d

4 Position the sleeve on the back of the quilt just below the top binding. Hand sew the sleeve in place along the long edges, leaving the ends open for inserting a hanging rod (**d**).

Labels

Please make a label for your quilt. It will be a reminder to you and to future generations; it's so easy to forget the date when we finished a quilt. It's sad that we do not know the makers of some of the wonderful antique quilts in museums and other collections. It's so much more interesting to know who made a quilt, when, where and in what circumstances. Your quilt may be a wedding gift or made to mark a graduation, the birth of a child, a coming of age or a birthday: record this information on the label.

There are various ways in which you can create a label. If you have access to a computer, one easy way is to print out the text using a font that you can trace. You can experiment with different layouts of the text before choosing a final idea and printing it out. Working on a light-box, tape the text in place. Back a piece of calico with freezer paper to stabilise the fabric while you are tracing; tape the fabric on top of the text, then trace the text with a Pigma™ 0.1pen. Remove the freezer paper. Turn under the raw edges of the calico label and hem it in place. This is a quick and easy label to make; you could make it more elaborate with additional appliqué, colour photographs printed onto fabric etc. It's also possible to buy blank printed fabric labels from quilt shops (**a**).

a

Final Thoughts

Creating a garden and making a quilt have many similarities. Both activities demand a great deal of our time, creative energy and patience. There has been a vogue in recent years for 'instant gardens' and TV make-over programmes, but these remove the essence of gardening – the delight of seeing the first blooms on a plant you have nurtured from seed; the seasonal changes creating different glorious colour combinations throughout the year; the satisfaction of combining different elements to create your own personal 'paradise.' So it is with stitching an appliqué quilt – except that we are not confined by seasons, climate and soil type.

We nurture our skills by practice – starting with simple shapes – until we are not daunted by the sharpest of points. Our simple flowers become gloriously multi-petalled and bloom with exuberance. We lay out our beautiful fabrics to determine the perfect colour combinations for a design. We observe the shading on petals and leaves as we make our selection with the aid of a pattern window. We combine a number of elements, such as trailing stems, dimensional details, embroidery and quilting to make a cohesive design. Finally we share the quilt with those we love in the same way that we like to share a garden with friends and family.

Both these activities take a while to reach fruition, but as the satisfaction is in the making, is there any need to hurry and to make speed the only criterion? In a fast-moving world it's rewarding to create something beautiful at our own pace – something perhaps to hand down to future generations. It's a luxury we deserve when we devote so much of our time and energy to making a quilt.

I hope you will be inspired by the ideas in this book to create your own beautiful Baltimore-style appliqué quilt.

About the Author

Shirley trained in textiles and design, and taught in high schools for 23 years. Her interest in hand appliqué - and Baltimore Album Quilts in particular - has led to a second career teaching workshops and residential courses throughout the UK as well as in the USA and France. Her designs are regularly featured in quilting magazines, and she publishes an appliqué pattern range called *Country Pleasures*.

Shirley lives with her husband (and three cats!) in a 500-year-old cottage in the heart of the unspoilt Suffolk countryside.

All the projects and samples in this book have been designed, hand appliquéd and quilted by Shirley.

Most of the photographs were taken in her cottage and garden.

Resources

YLI™ silk threads, Clover™ appliqué pins and Clover™ white marking pens are available from many quilt shops including:

Sew & So's
14, Upper Olland Street, Bungay, Suffolk NR35 1BG (www.sewsos.co.uk) (also mail order)

Sew Creative
Wroxham Barns, Tunstead Road, Hoveton, Norfolk NR12 8QU

Overlay material is available from the above two shops

Straw #11 needles are available from Sew & So's

Mylar™ circles are available from Brandy's (www.brandysquiltpatterns.com) and Creative Grids (www.creativegrids.com). Karen Kay Buckley produces a wide range of circles called Perfect Circles™ (www.karenkaybuckley.com).

Shirley gives talks on the history of Baltimore Album Quilts and her own interpretation – Baltimore with an English flavour – illustrated with many examples of her work. She teaches a number of one-day hand appliqué workshops based on her designs, as well as longer courses. See her website for further details, or write to her at Nightingales, Lindsey, Ipswich, Suffolk, England IP7 6PP.

Shirley also publishes a range of appliqué designs and quilt patterns. The block designs are the same size as those in this book, and can be combined to make larger quilts in your own arrangements. You can obtain a catalogue of her patterns by sending an SAE to the same address. Order direct from her at www.shirleybloomfield.co.uk, or from the shops below.

UK
Sew & So's and Sew Creative (see above)

USA
Hickory Hill Quilt Bus
www.HickoryHillQuilts.com
(this is an on-line and mobile quilt business)

Pennington Quilt Works
www.penningtonquilts.com, New Jersey

Quilt Adventures
www.quiltadventures.com
(on-line specialist appliqué supplies)

The Village Quilter, Mount Holly, New Jersey
www.millraceshops.com

Further Reading

Elly Sienkiewicz has written many books on Baltimore Album Quilts; they are published by C & T Publishing, PO Box 1456, Lafayette, CA 94549

OAK AND ACORN PAPERCUT TEMPLATE

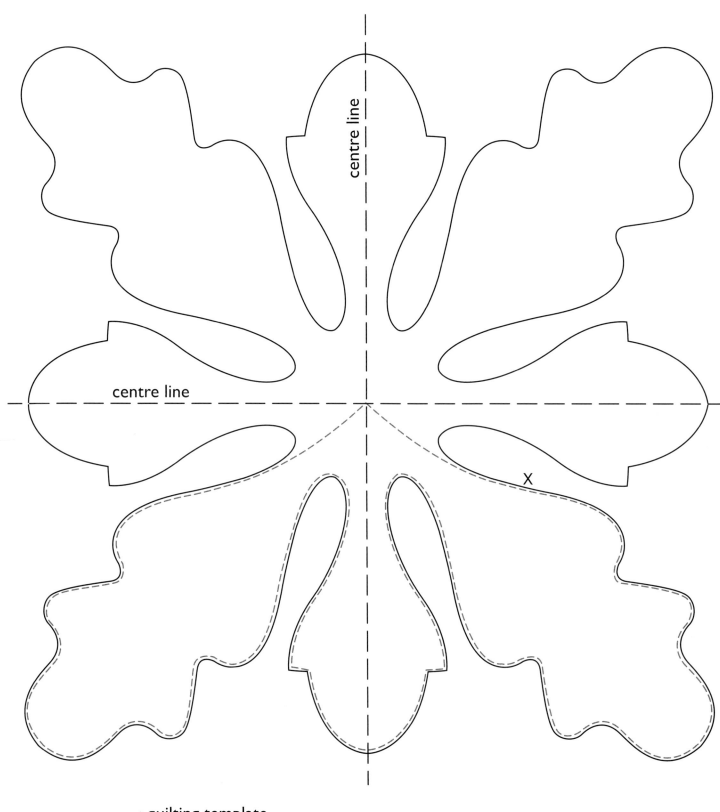

centre line

centre line

X

quilting template

The Appliqué Garden

APPLES DESIGN AND TEMPLATES

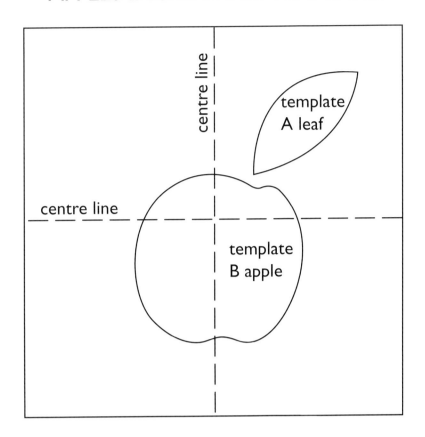

FLOWER FACES TEMPLATES

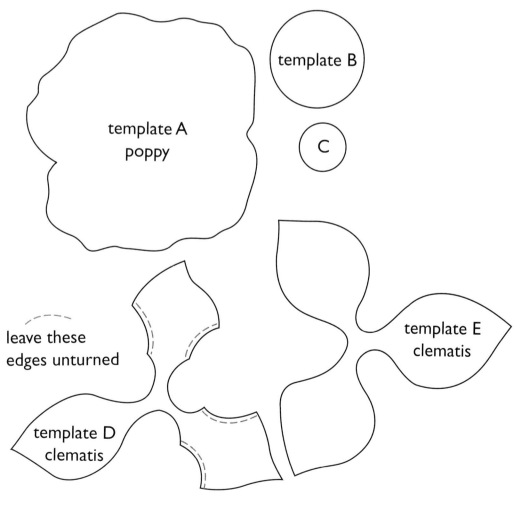

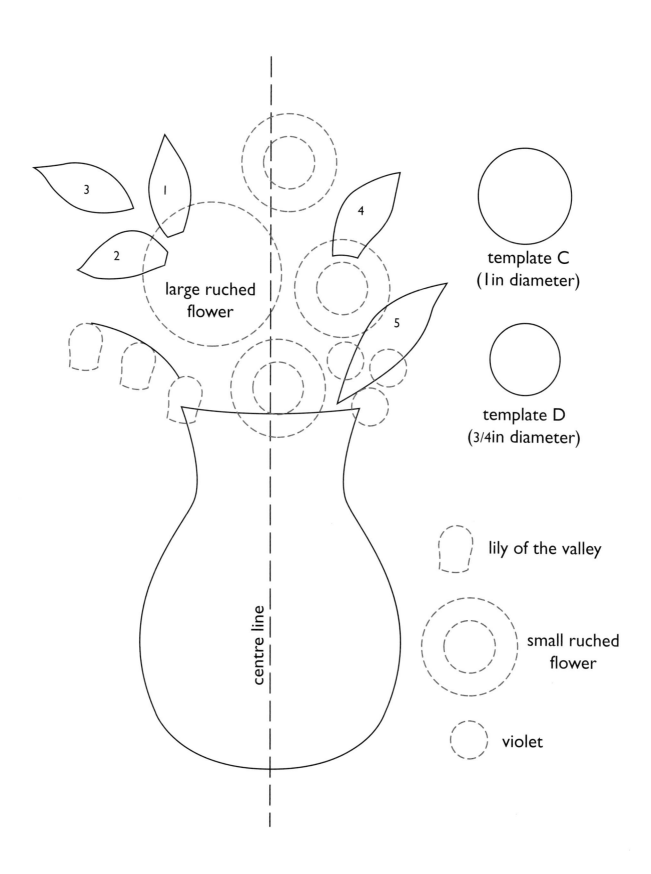

large ruched flower

template C
(1in diameter)

template D
(3/4in diameter)

lily of the valley

small ruched flower

violet

centre line

CYCLAMEN DESIGN
AND TEMPLATES

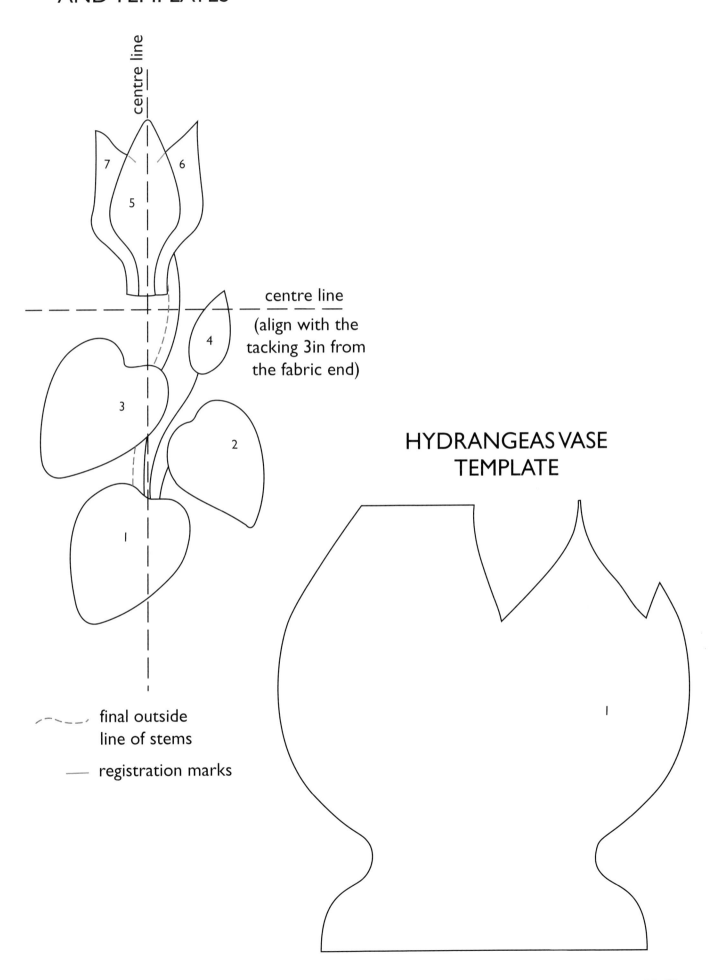

centre line

7   6

5

centre line

(align with the
tacking 3in from
the fabric end)

4

3

2

HYDRANGEAS VASE
TEMPLATE

1

1

final outside
line of stems

registration marks

1

HYDRANGEAS DESIGN A

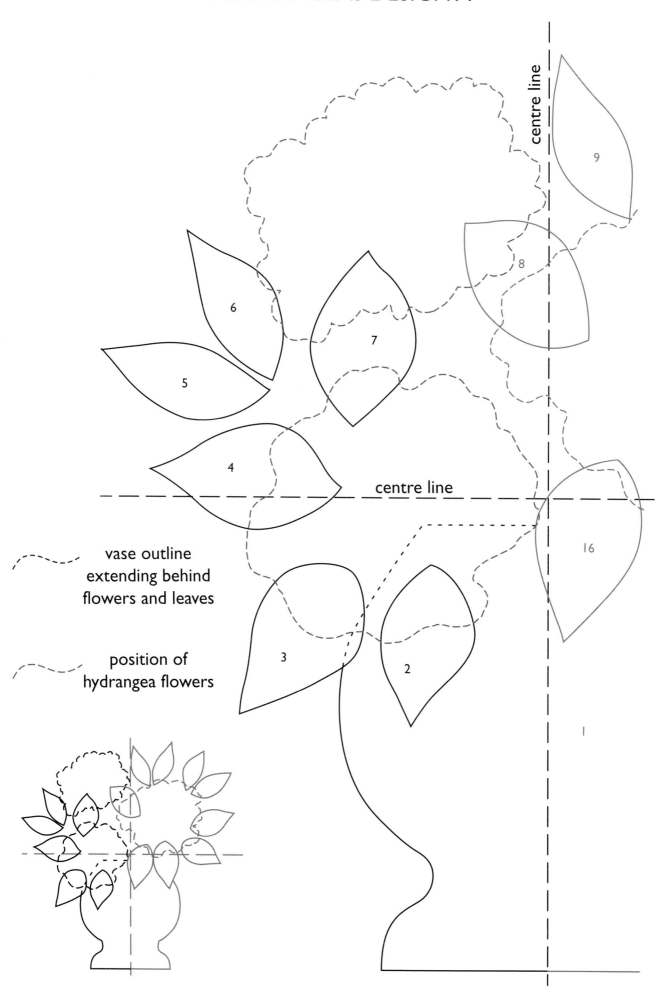

centre line

centre line

vase outline
extending behind
flowers and leaves

position of
hydrangea flowers

5

6

7

8

9

4

3

2

16

1

HYDRANGEAS DESIGN B

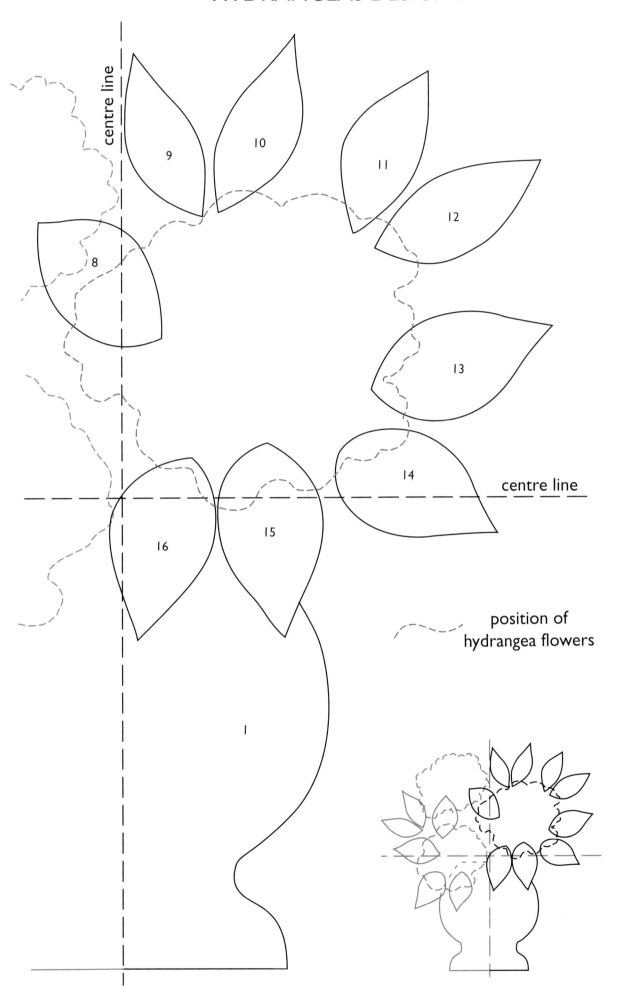

centre line

9

10

11

12

8

13

14

centre line

16

15

1

position of
hydrangea flowers

AUTUMN GLORY DESIGN A

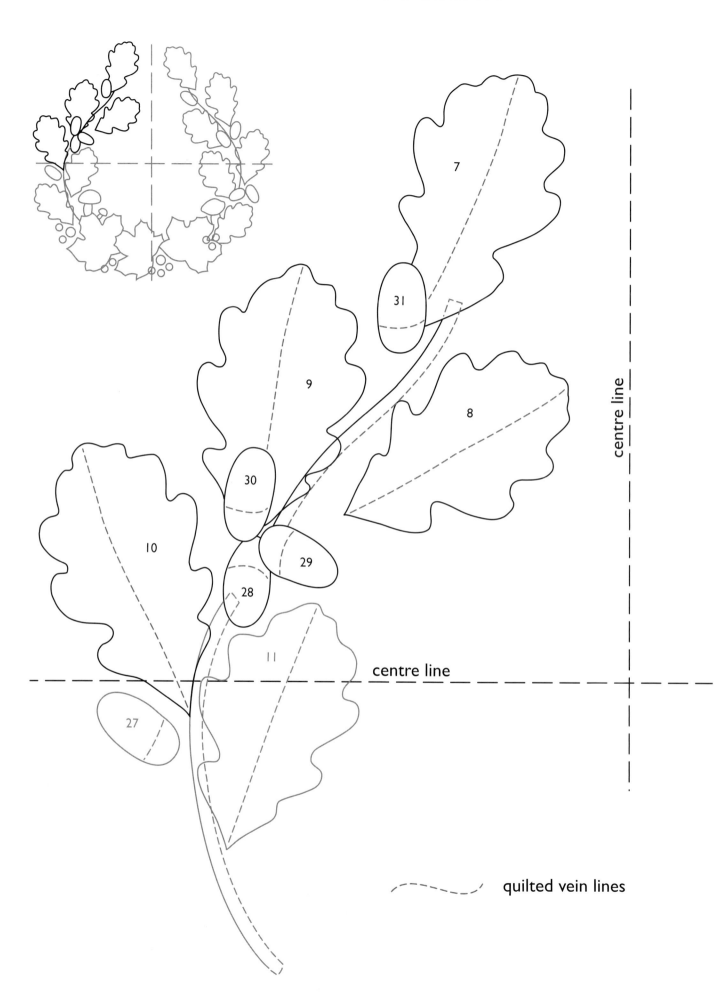

centre line

centre line

7

31

9

8

30

29

28

10

11

27

quilted vein lines

AUTUMN GLORY DESIGN B

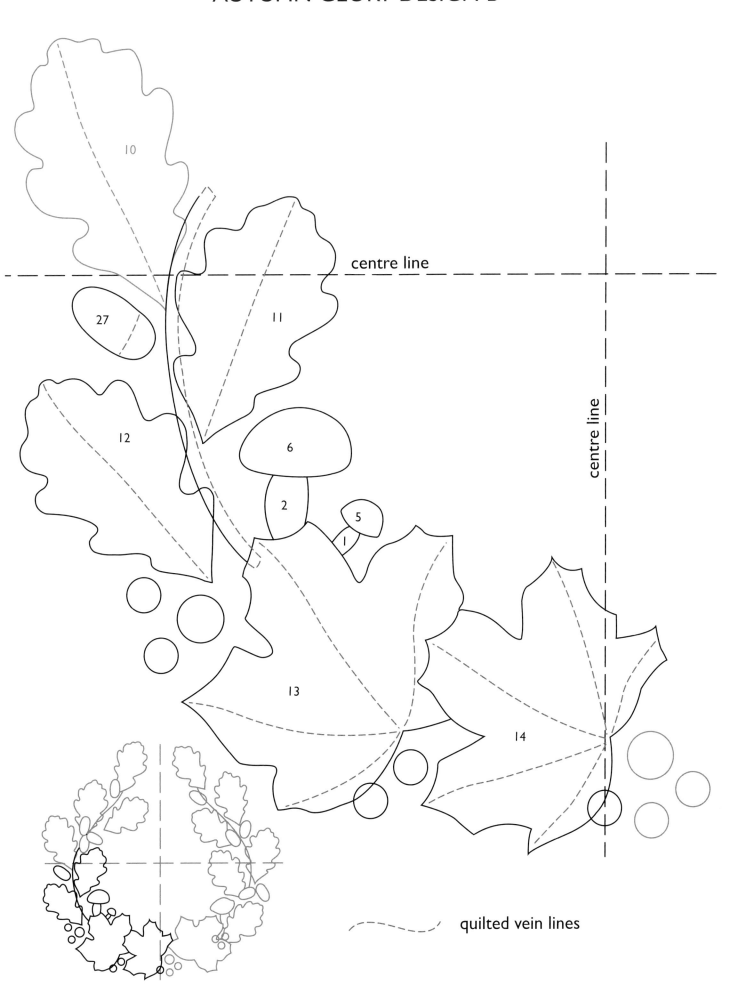

centre line

centre line

10

27

11

12

6

2

5

1

13

14

quilted vein lines

AUTUMN GLORY DESIGN C

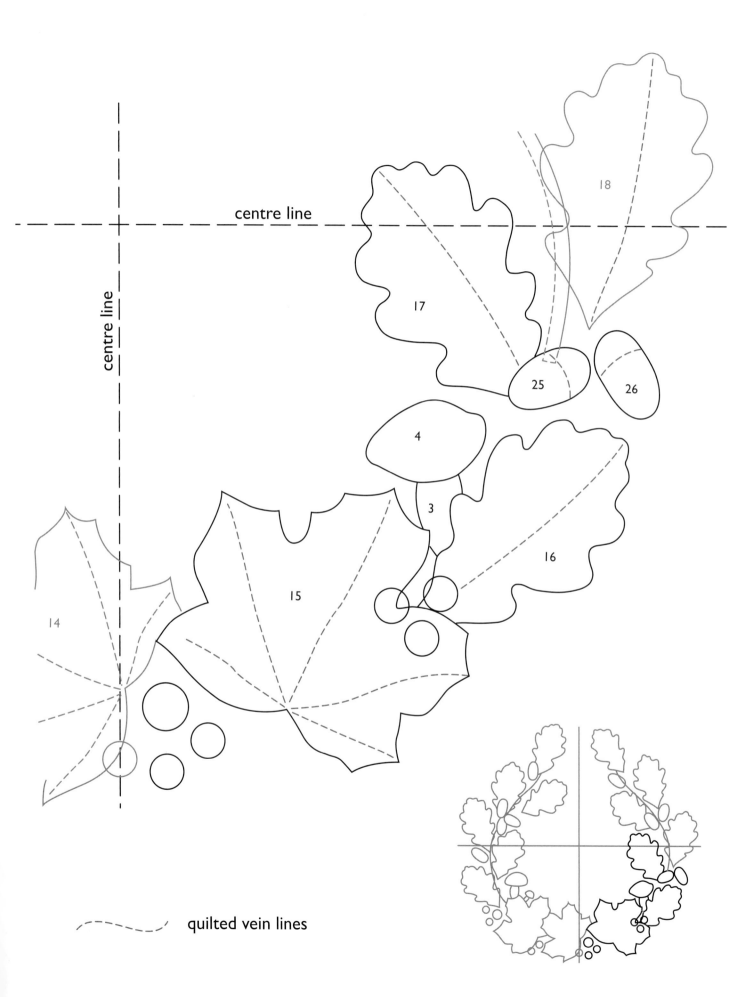

centre line

18

17

25

26

4

3

16

15

14

quilted vein lines

The Appliqué Garden

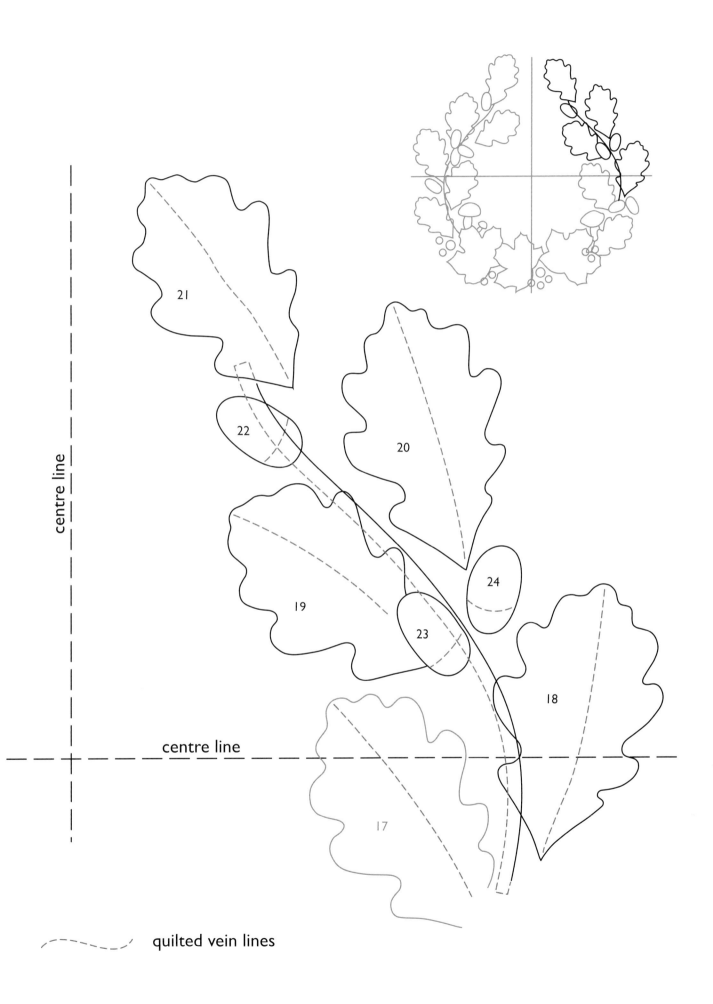

centre line

centre line

21

22

20

19

24

23

18

17

quilted vein lines

finished length D

AUTUMN GLORY
BORDER TEMPLATES

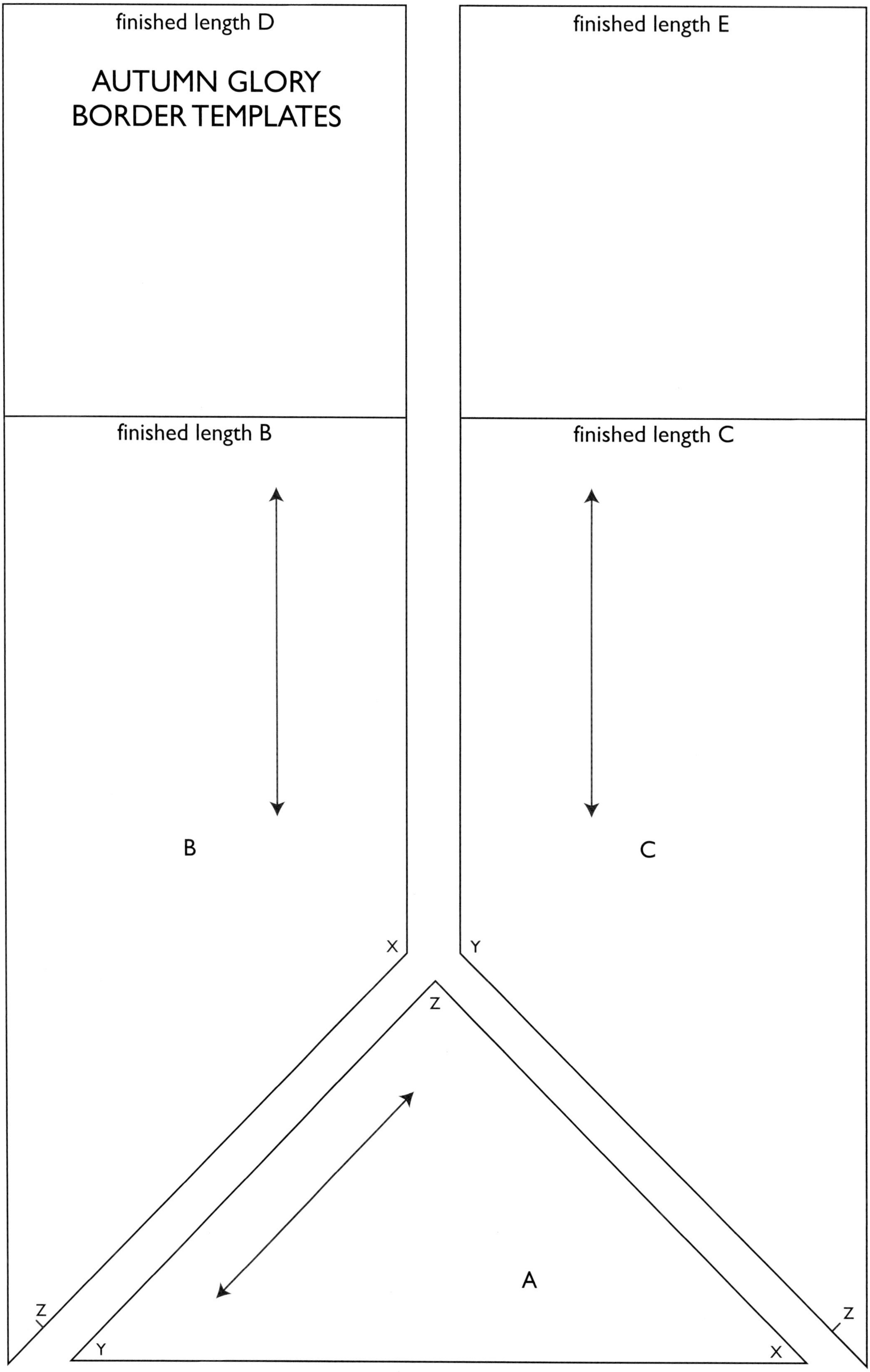

finished length E

finished length B

finished length C

add 1/4in seam allowance throughout

B

C

X

Y

Z

Z

Z

A

Z

Y

X

AUTUMN GLORY QUILTED BORDER DESIGN

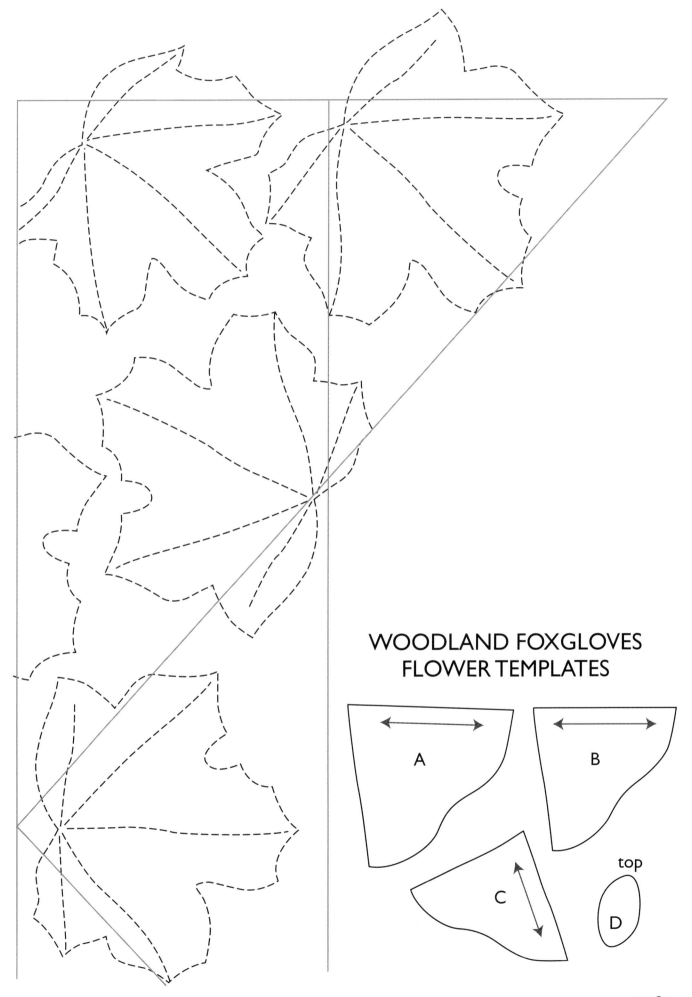

WOODLAND FOXGLOVES
FLOWER TEMPLATES

A

B

C

top

D

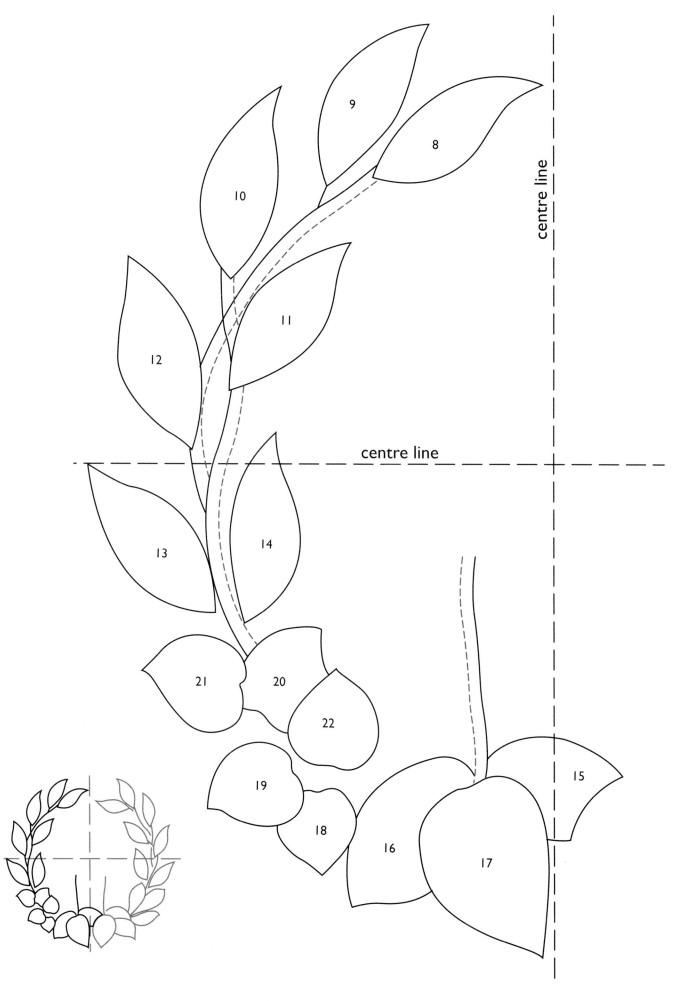

centre line

centre line

WOODLAND FOXGLOVES DESIGN B

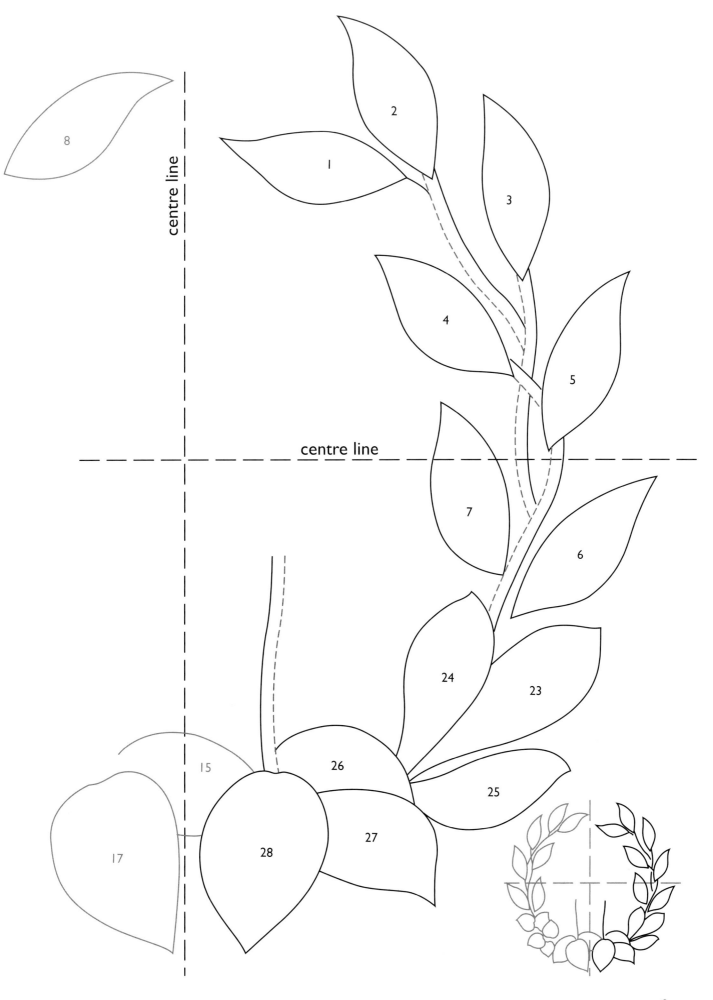

centre line

centre line

8

1

2

3

4

5

7

6

24

23

15

26

25

17

28

27

NASTURTIUMS DESIGN A

centre line

centre line

Template A
bud

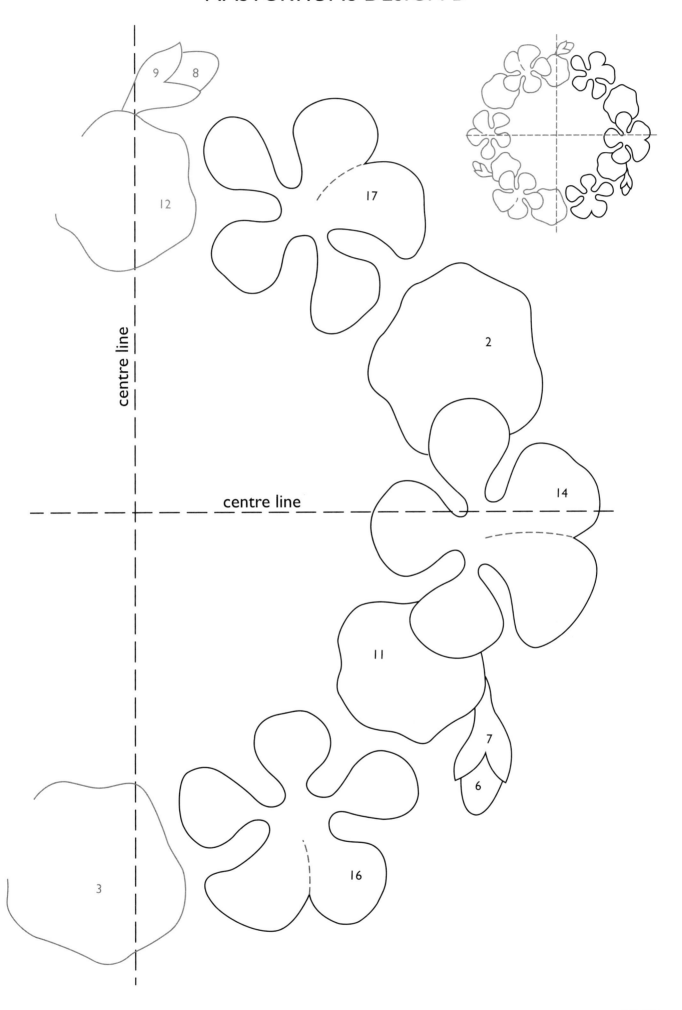

9

8

12

17

2

centre line

centre line

14

11

7

6

3

16

DAISY CHAIN DESIGN A

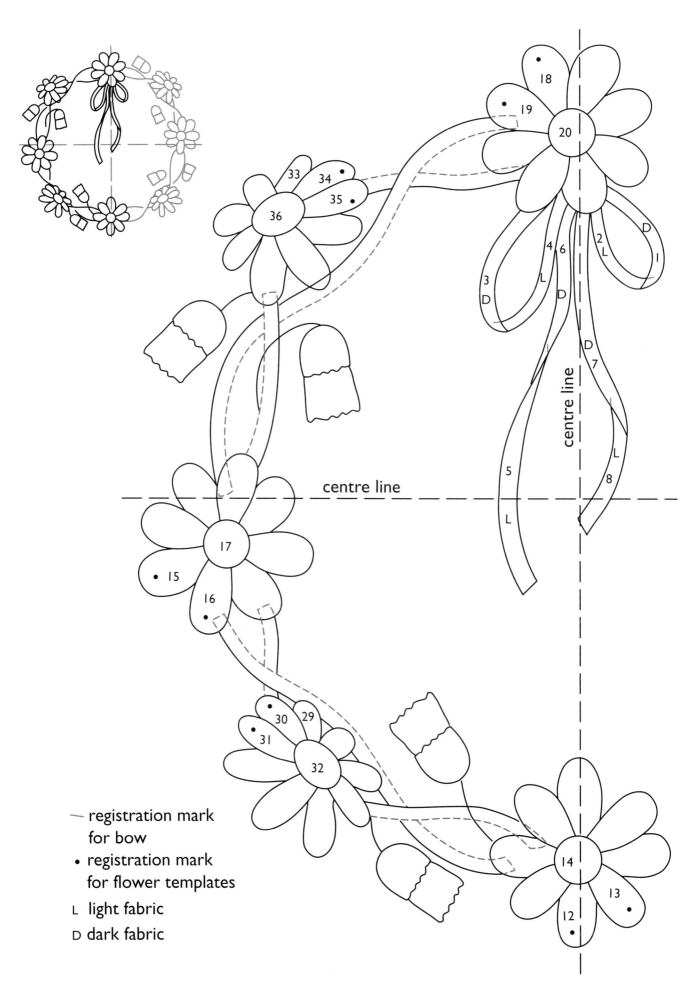

— registration mark
   for bow
• registration mark
   for flower templates
L light fabric
D dark fabric

The Appliqué Garden

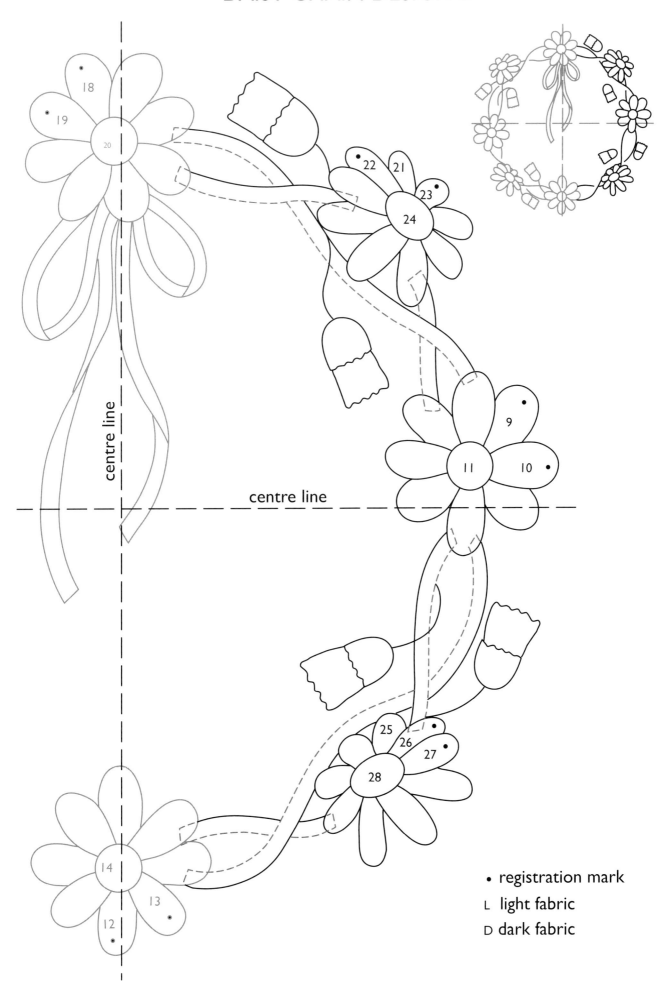

- registration mark
- L light fabric
- D dark fabric

DAISY CHAIN FLOWER TEMPLATES

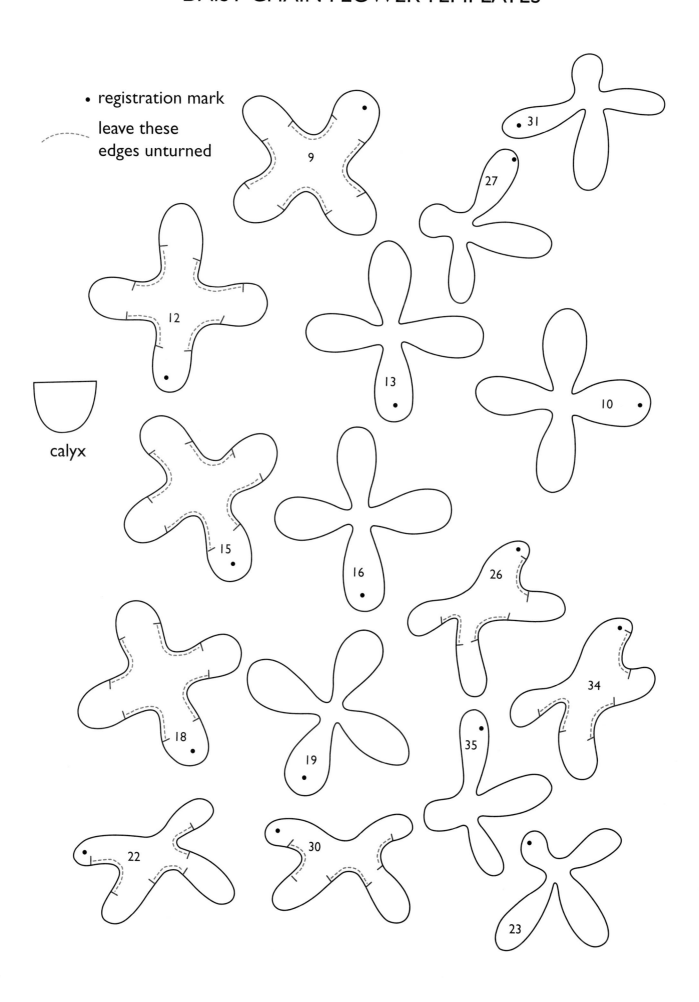

- registration mark
- leave these edges unturned

calyx

The Appliqué Garden

SUMMER BOUNTY EXTRA TEMPLATES

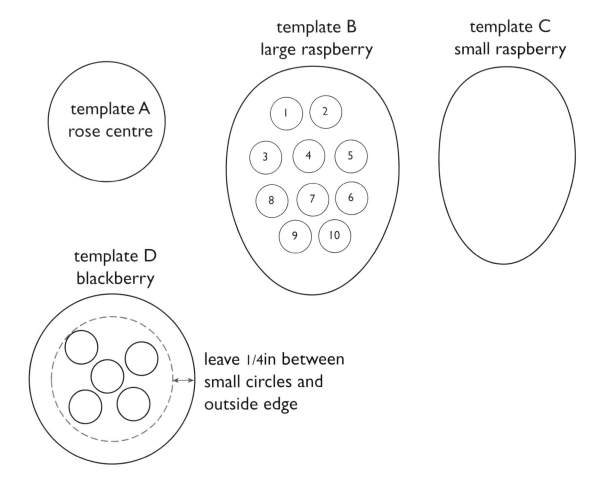

template A
rose centre

template B
large raspberry

template C
small raspberry

template D
blackberry

leave 1/4in between small circles and outside edge

FLOWERS WITH DIMENSION TEMPLATES

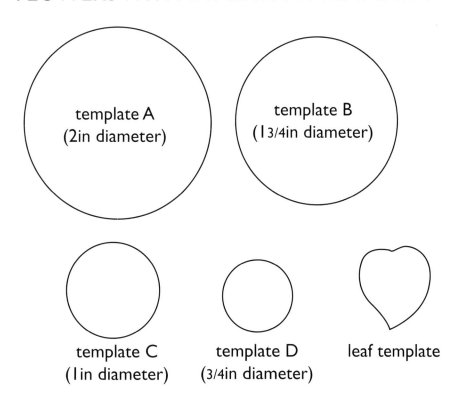

template A
(2in diameter)

template B
(1 3/4in diameter)

template C
(1in diameter)

template D
(3/4in diameter)

leaf template

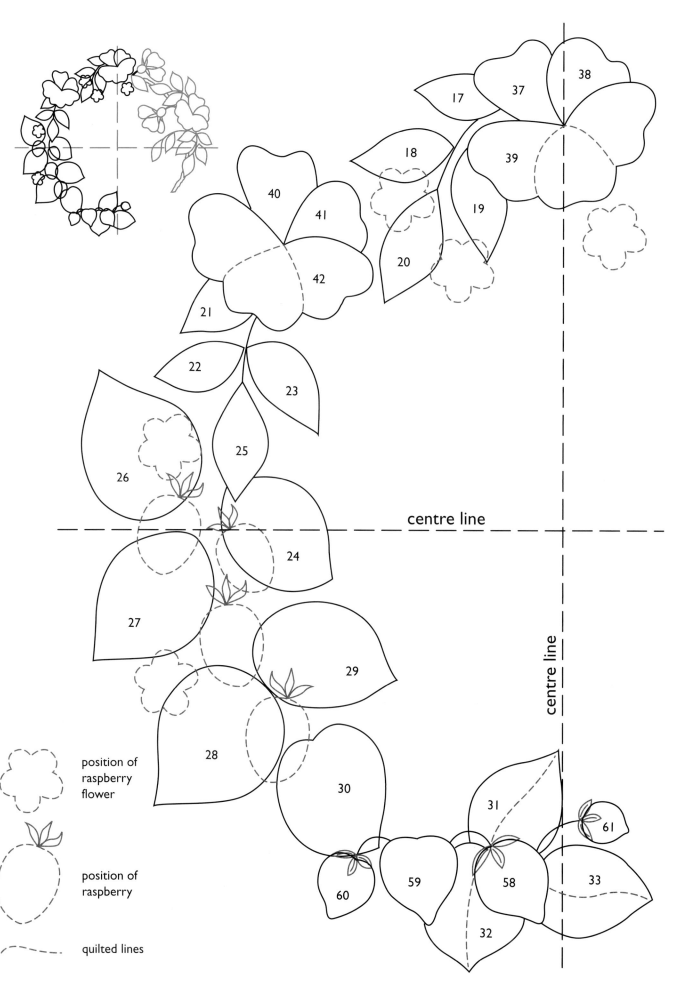

position of
raspberry
flower

position of
raspberry

quilted lines

centre line

centre line

SUMMER BOUNTY DESIGN B

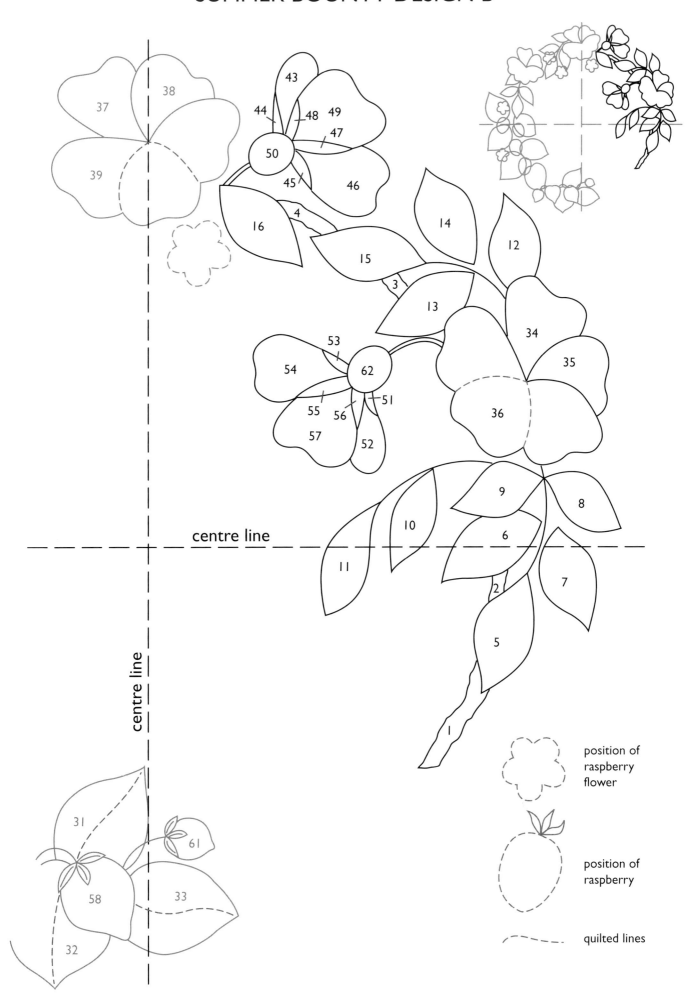

37
38
39

43
44
48 49
47
50
45
46
4
16
15
3
13

14
12

centre line

54
53
62
51
55
56
52
57

34
35
36

centre line

9
10
8
6
11
7
2
5
1

31
61
58
33
32

position of
raspberry
flower

position of
raspberry

quilted lines

WOODPECKER DESIGN A

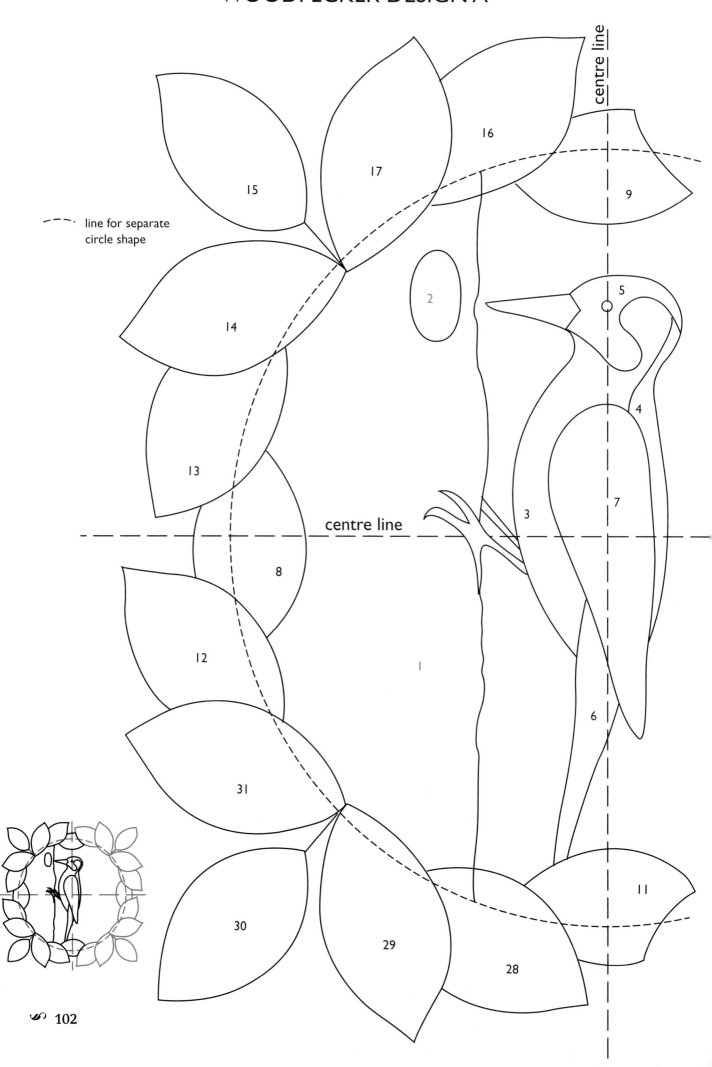

centre line

line for separate circle shape

15

17

16

9

centre line

2

5

14

4

13

3

7

8

1

12

6

31

30

29

28

11

WOODPECKER DESIGN B

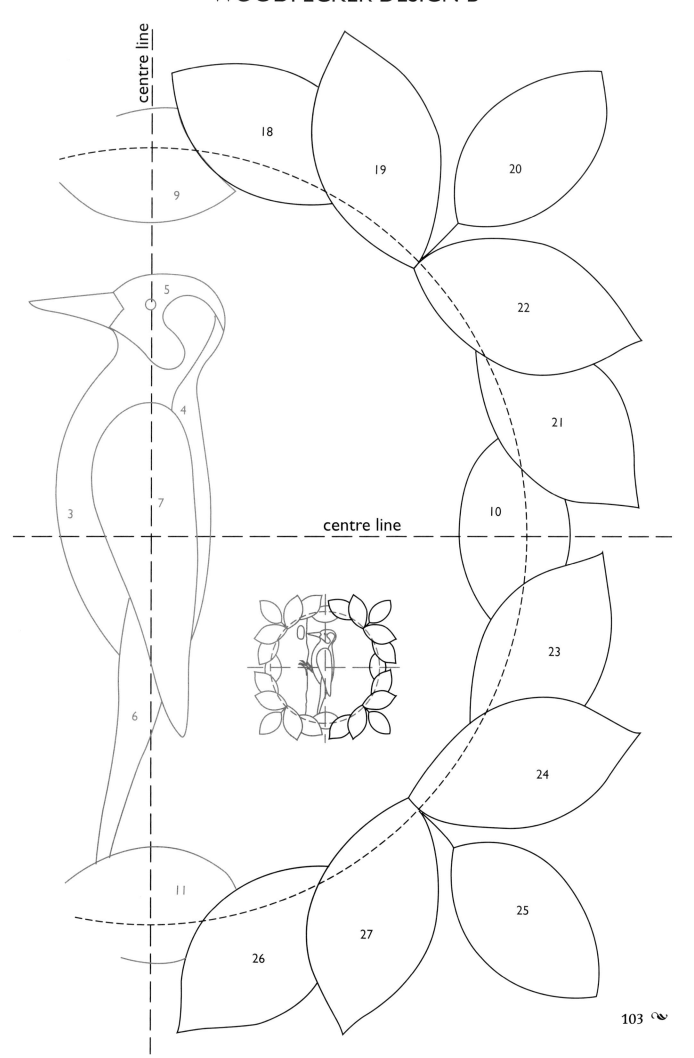

centre line

centre line

18

19

20

9

5

4

22

21

3

7

10

6

23

24

11

26

27

25

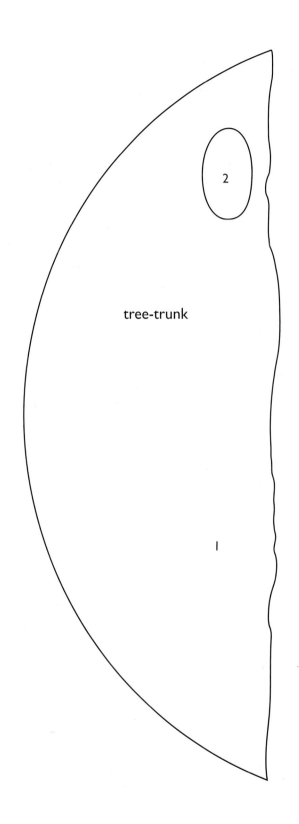

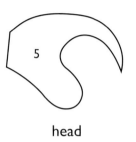

head